ROMAN SOLDIERS DON'T
WEAR WATCHES

ROMAN SOLDIERS DON'T WEAR WATCHES

333 Film Flubs—Memorable Movie Mistakes

BILL GIVENS

A CITADEL PRESS BOOK
PUBLISHED BY CAROL PUBLISHING GROUP

For Mary Wickes, whose comedy brought joy to generations, who honored me with her friendship, and whose memory I cherish; and for Bill Kendall, who taught me that the best movies usually have words at the bottom of the screen, and whose courage overcame the tyranny of small-minded preachers, politicians, and film censors

A Citadel Press Book
Published by Carol Publishing Group
Citadel Press is a registered trademark of Carol Communications, Inc.

Editorial, sales and distribution, rights and permissions inquiries should be addressed to Carol Publishing Group, 120 Enterprise Avenue, Secaucus, N.J. 07094

In Canada: Canadian Manda Group, One Atlantic Avenue, Suite 105, Toronto, Ontario M6K 3E7

Carol Publishing Group books may be purchased in bulk at special discounts for sales promotion, fund-raising, or educational purposes. Special editions can be created to specifications. For details, contact Special Sales Department, 120 Enterprise Avenue, Secaucus, N.J. 07094.

Manufactured in the United States of America

10   9   8   7   6   5   4   3   2   1

Library of Congress Cataloging-in-Publication Data
Givens, Bill.
        Roman soldiers don't wear watches : 333 film flubs—memorable movie mistakes / Bill Givens.
            p.   cm.
        "A Citadel Press book."
        ISBN 0-8065-1829-4 (pb)
        1. Motion picture errors. I. Title.
PN1994.9G589   1996
791.43—dc20   96-46056
                                                             CIP

CONTENTS

PREFACE

Sometimes, things just get out of hand. When the first *Film Flubs* book was published in 1990, like most authors, I had hopes of a moderate success, but had no idea that it would become a best-seller, would spawn three sequels, be published in Europe, and now be compiled with the other *Film Flubs* books and updated in this volume. I hoped for one or two publicity interviews; never could I have imagined that it would lead to appearances on virtually every entertainment-related television show in the U.S., features in every major metropolitan newspaper, a plethora of magazine articles, lectures on university campuses, and literally hundreds of radio interviews in the United States, Canada, Great Britain, and Australia.

Most gratifying of all, I never envisioned the reader response. When we put an address in the first book for readers to write and share their favorite flubs, again I would have been grateful for an occasional letter. I was totally unprepared for the reader response, and will probably never be able to adequately acknowledge the contributions you made to this and to the earlier editions. Within days after *Film Flubs* appeared in the bookstores, the mail started to come in by the bushel. Thousands upon thousands of you have written in to share your favorite film goofs, and many have gone to the trouble of submitting large, painstakingly re-searched lists. I never imagined that world-famous actors, directors, writers, producers, and film crew members would be so willing to share their favorite flubs, even ones which appeared in their own films.

In earlier books, we attempted to acknowledge your contributions with "Flub Spotter Squad," and hope to do so again in the future. However, since this book includes material from *Film Flubs, Son of Film Flubs,* and *Film Flubs: The Sequel*—as well as flubs from films which appeared since *Film Flubs: The Sequel* was published, it's just impossible to do so. Early on, when the books were first published, we might hear about a flub from only one person, perhaps two or three. Now it's not at all unusual to begin getting letters about flubs before the film leaves the theaters, and to hear from a host of loyal *Film Flubs* readers simultaneously reporting the same gaffe. We're going to figure out a way to acknowledge your contributions, as well as your kindness in taking the time to write and share your favorites. And don't worry, the "Sharp-Eyes, Quick-Witted Flub Spotter Squad" will return.

Writing is a solitary experience, and nothing cheers the heart of a scribe more than hearing that his work has engendered a laugh, brightened a dull day, or cheered someone during an attack of *weltschmerz* (look it up for yourself!). I'm gratified that these books have done that for so many of you, and know that your letters have done the same for me. Every day there are at least one or two letters from *Film Flubs* readers in the mail. Some are quick notes, some are elaborate lists. All are deeply appreciated, and hopefully I'll be able to respond to them. However, the Film Flubs Organization to which some of you have written is but one man, a keyboard and a warm seat in the back of a darkened theater, so please know how much I appreciate your sharing even if I have not been able to respond.

We're moving forward with technology, and soon there will be an opportunity to share favorite flubs from the very latest movies on the Internet. Look for it with your Web browser in the near future.

We look forward to having your name in future editions as part of the Flub Spotter Squad. The mailing address to share your favorite goofs, gaffes, flubs, and inside jokes is:

Film Flubs
7510 Sunset Boulevard, #551
Hollywood, California 90046-3418

Enjoy!

INTRODUCTION

In previous books in the series, we discussed at length the hows and whys of film flubbery and the causes for their ultimate appearance on the screen. Rather than tread the same ground again, we commend the previous tomes to your attention (now there's a sneaky way to sell books!). In each we've tried to look at some aspect of the factors which make things go awry on films. However, there are topics which should bear discussion.

Film flubs can be more than the physical glitches which you see on screen. To many of us who have some subjective interest, anything that pulls us away from the story on the screen and into reality can, in truth, be classified as a flub.

My personal *bête noir* is botched accents, especially Southern ones. As a former Southerner who hasn't quite lost the sound, I groan, gripe, and grind my teeth when I see some ill-prepared actor try to fit a "grits and gravy" Southern accent into a mouth which can't quite hold it. I'd rather see them go for their own natural speech pattern. Adding insult to injury is the refuge of the brain-dead filmmaker who uses a Southern accent as the cliché to telegraph stupid, racist, or less than savory characters. I'm sure the folks from Brooklyn have to endure similar anguish.

Another personal gripe is the way presents are wrapped in movies and television shows. Perhaps to avoid rewraps for take after take, a gift given cinematically usually has a beribboned lid wrapped separately from the bottom, so it slides off carefully. In real life, of course, we rip, tear, and crumple the wrapping paper and box to get to the gift. We've never given nor received gifts wrapped as they are on film.

Elizabeth Taylor is the queen of bad Southern accents—see *Cat on a Hot Tin Roof* (1958) or *Raintree County* (1957) as examples. Joe Pesci's Southern accent in *JFK* (1991) is so bad that you want to laugh at the parts which really aren't funny—and Kevin Costner's in the same film is such a distraction that you wonder if he has a clue about vocal technique (see also *Robin Hood*). New Orleans residents were not amused when Costner's *JFK* accent wasn't theirs with its Cajun overtones, but a drawl more common to Mississippi and Alabama.

Another big-time annoyance is the constant use of wet streets in night shots—especially in films taking place in Los Angeles. I know why they do it—the shiny surface makes for better reflections and a more pleasing shot. But as a Los Angeles resident, I have to tell you that the streets here are wet probably less than ten nights a year. Every time I see damp pavement in a scene set in L.A., my attention is diverted from the on-screen story.

While I'm on the shrink's couch, indulge me as I point out one other filmic technique which bugs me, even though it's certainly not a flub. But is it possible to end a movie without a traditional pullback, the camera moving into a panoramic view of the scene as our heroes walk, run, drive, fly, ride on horseback, or stumble into the horizon? There's almost always a road in the shot, heading straight over a slight rise into infinity. Is this something that directors learn, with the technique being passed down from one generation to another, or is it merely a colossal lack of imagination? Your call.

Misplaced geography is another bothersome distraction, especially to one living in the area where a movie was filmed. You may not have noticed the pan from downtown L.A. to downtown San Francisco in *The*

Doctor (see page 29), but many of us Los Angeleans were jarred by it. In the same vein, we didn't notice the geographic blunders in *No Way Out* (page 31), but Washingtonians did, being especially bugged by Costner's use of a Georgetown MetroRail station. There's no station in Georgetown. But again, it's hard to classify these as flubs, since location shooting has its own set of exigencies. Many times, license must be taken.

Nonetheless, Austrians were amused when *The Sound of Music* (1965) was first shown in their country, because as the Von Trapp family made its way across the mountains to freedom, in reality they were heading straight into Nazi Germany.

Then again, location gaffes are not endemic to the movies. In the opera *Manon Lescaut*, Puccini exiles his heroine to the desert just outside New Orleans. Go find it—or go figure.

Yet another on-screen flub that has bothered me for years is the camera's iris reflection—that little pentagram that flashes onto the screen when the camera is pointed directly at the sun. I'm happy to report that I have a cohort in this one. Allan Provost wrote to *The Hollywood Reporter* to kvetch about the same subject, putting it succinctly: "Why is it that so many filmmakers allow sunspots, dramatic streaks of light and even the concentric circles caused by the camera to dominate scenes? The effect is the same as seeing the microphone boom: It reminds the viewer of the technology and ruins the sense of involvement."

We especially enjoyed his reflection (oops! unintentional pun) on *Black Robe* which, he says, "has gone to great lengths to create the sense of looking at a bygone world and then, by golly, ending it with the visible lens, reminding me that my intense concern for the cold and starving

Indians was unfounded, since they were just a short distance away from the jelly doughnuts of the nearest catering truck."

A reader pointed out something which never occurred to us, but now that we think about it—j'ever notice that in movies, almost everyone at the on-screen funeral wears black, whereas in real life, hardly anyone does these days? And that frequently, there's a carved tombstone in place before the body's even cold? Yet another cinematic cliché.

End of sermon. Pass the plate. Let the flubbing begin.

COSTUME CHANGES

At London's Elstree Studios, prim Elaine Scheyreck faced quite a dilemma. As a costumer, she spent plenty of time in the company of actors who were stripped down to their bare essentials—still, she was faced with something she preferred not to discuss. Just back from viewing the dailies of *Superman*, Ms. Scheyreck now had to tell the producers that a scene had to be re-shot because Christopher Reeve's "private parts" jumped from one side to the other in his tight-fitting costume.

Had the error not been caught and corrected, somewhere along the way audiences would have had a real laugh—probably at a most inappropriate time—when Reeve's goodies flew from one side to the other in mid-scene.

From that day forward, one of Elaine Scheyreck's duties was to make sure that the handsome actor's pants bulge was in the right place every day—and since multiple costume changes were required because Reeve would get sweaty during the complex flying scenes, it was finally decided to eliminate the problem completely by having a "swim cup" sewn into the Superman outfits.

Where's Your Point?

Brad Pitt wears his collar outside his sweater as he sits in a restaurant booth in *A River Runs Through It* (1992). Several times throughout the scene the point of the collar is either inside or outside the sweater.

Disorder in the Court

When Glenn Close and Jeff Bridges enter the courtroom in *Jagged Edge* (1985), she is wearing a gray suit. Then she makes her opening arguments standing before the judge wearing a dark blue suit and a white blouse. A few minutes later (without having time to go home and change), she questions a witness while wearing a dark brown suit and a light brown blouse.

How's That Again, Sam?

After more than forty-six years of being one of history's most-watched movies, no one seemed to notice that the wardrobe department blew it when they dressed Ingrid Bergman for a flashback scene in *Casablanca* (1942). Bergman's Ilsa remembers wearing a dress when she and Bogart's Rick parted months before in Paris. But when Ted Turner's perspicacious colorizers got a closer look at the film, they discovered that Ilsa was actually wearing a suit.

"I never noticed that, and I've seen that film many times," Turner Entertainment President Roger Mayer, who supervised the colorization process, told the *Los Angeles Times*. "I don't think many people would." But somebody did.

He Knocked the Polka Dots Right Off His Tie

Humphrey Bogart backhands Peter Lorre in *The Maltese Falcon* (1941). When Lorre's head snaps left, he's wearing a polka-dot bow tie. When it snaps back to the right, he's wearing a striped one.

The Little Tramp and His Wandering Hat

Charlie Chaplin couldn't keep up with his trademark hat in *The Vagabond* (1916). When the Little Tramp is being chased around and through a bar, he falls and loses his hat outside the place but when he enters again he's wearing it. He then exits once more, hatless, and outside picks up the hat off the sidewalk where he originally dropped it.

Charlie's hat problems continue when he rescues a gypsy girl, and her father tries to drown him in a washtub. He escapes soaking wet and hatless, and jumps onto the back of a wagon, spitting water in the father's face. In the next shot, he's climbing into the front of the wagon, not only wearing the hat, but bone dry.

Unexpected Modesty

There's not an excess of modesty in the porn business, as explored in *Hardcore* (1979), but shortly after she's seen totally nude in a peep booth, Season Hubley's panties appear.

Unexpected Modesty II: The Adventure Continues

Another bit of undergarment prestidigitation takes place in *National Lampoon's Animal House* (1978) when Tim Matheson is kissing and fondling a girl in a car. As he lifts her top off it's clear that she is wearing no bra. When his pals come out of the Dexter Lake Club, she screams and jumps out, wearing nothing but her skirt and shoes. But when she lands in the car next to her, a bra has magically appeared.

The Hot Foot

Mary Stuart Masterson lights a tissue in *Benny & Joon* (1993) and Aidan Quinn stomps it out wearing sneakers. But moments later he's wearing oxfords when he flushes a dead goldfish down the toilet.

Cathy and Heathcliffe Went Up the Hill...

Heading up the hill to meet Heathcliffe in *Wuthering Heights* (1939), Merle Oberon's Cathy drapes a shawl over her shoulders. She is wearing a blouse and a full-length skirt. Somewhere between the bottom of the hill and the top, she must have found a dressing room and changed clothes— or stopped off and left the clothes she was wearing at the Moor-side cleaners. When she reaches the top where her brooding lover waits, she's wearing an entirely different, tailored dress and no shawl.

Sarong Collection

Loni Anderson finds herself marooned on a desert island with Perry King and a teeny-weeny overnight case in the TV movie *Stranded* (1986), but the teeny-weeny case manages to provide her with not only enough shades of blush for a year's worth of intimate candlelight rendezvous but also an amazing assortment of revealing sarongs. (And she was only on a quick business trip.)

God Help the Script Girl

The Beatles wear different clothing from one shot to another in the opening dash-onto-the-train sequence of *A Hard Day's Night* (1964). The "why" of the moment has been preserved for posterity by continuity supervisor Rita Davison. Her notes for the shot, as quoted by Peter Van Gelder in *That's Hollywood*, say: "First shot taken while I was in the ladies' toilet. I think they were the Beatles, but they were wearing the clothing which they came in with, and not what was supposed to be worn. It was photographed by the director. I trust this is not the way we intend to go on. God help me."

The Leaky Space Suit

Dave Bowen's space suit isn't very airtight in a shot in *2001: A Space Odyssey* (1968). When he reenters the Discovery spaceship with its atmosphere evacuated, he opens an access hatch to the HAL 9000 logic center and climbs over the camera into the chamber wearing his E.V.A. airtight space suit. As his left hand moves past, the glove separates from the sleeve, showing his bare wrist.

And hey, you want to have a little fun? Think about the name of the computer: HAL. Then think about the letter that follows each in the alphabet. Arthur Clarke said it was just a coincidence.

Shot to Shot, Shoe to Shoe

At the ending of *Above the Law* (1988), Steven Seagal is fighting a group of terrorists in a grocery store. As the police cars approach, he grabs one of the thugs and uses him as a shield to crash through the store's front window. He leaps forward wearing black leather boots but lands on the sidewalk in Reebok tennis shoes.

Sneakering Through the Window

Similarly, in *The First Power* (1990), Lou Diamond Phillips wears silver-tipped cowboy boots throughout most of the movie. When he climbs through a church window he's wearing sneakers which then become cowboy boots again when he jumps out the window and runs down the street.

She Wasn't in Much of a Hurry

Vicki Vale (Kim Basinger) is told about the Wayne family tragedy in *Batman* (1989). She rushes to see Bruce Wayne, but somewhere along the way she must have stopped off to spruce up, because she arrives in a different dress and hairstyle.

The $330 Loss

Kim Basinger wants to purchase a $300 scarf at a flea market in *9¹/₂ Weeks* (1986). But she takes a wiser course and buys instead a $30 set of ducks, which she puts into a shopping bag. Mickey Rourke then surprises her with the scarf and drapes it over her shoulders. They walk to the waterfront, but by the time they get there, she's neither wearing the scarf nor carrying the shopping bag.

Tied to Be Fit

Sam Waterston can't keep up with his tie in a scene from Woody Allen's *September* (1987). The movie has much to do with the expression of angst during a weekend in Vermont (has there ever been a Woody Allen movie *sans* angst?). Waterston's is so severe that during a conversation with Jack Warden, his necktie is alternately tied and untied at regular intervals.

In and Out of the Dark

In *JFK* (1991), when in a restaurant with Kevin Costner, John Candy stands up from the table wearing his sunglasses. In the next shot, his hat is in his hand, but there are no sunglasses anywhere. Then when he puts the hat on his head, he's wearing shades again.

Similarly, in *Beverly Hills Cop II* (1987), Eddie Murphy as Alex Foley gets into a fight with a guard at a warehouse. Taking a punch, the guard's sunglasses fly off his face. After a few seconds of struggle with Murphy, he's wearing them again.

Terminator II: Judgment Day

In each book, we award the "Flubbie" to a movie which earns the dubious distinction of "Flubbed-Up Movie of the Year." In 1990, it was *Pretty Woman*. The 1991 award was won hands-down by *Terminator II: Judgment Day*.

As a bit of a caveat, having read much about the making of *T2*, we have to admit that as one of filmdom's great displays of special effects wizardry, it was a real bear to make—and the wonder is that it did get put together, and that it does work. The efforts of hundreds of technicians from dozens of companies had to come together in one motion picture, and that there is any continuity at all is a tribute to the film-makers. But, as Marc Antony said, we did not come here to praise. Our task is to point out flubs, and we shall not shirk it.

Early on, a couple of flubs pop up. When Arnie is heading toward the bar, he passes a car parked outside. His cranial read-out says that the car he's scanning is a Plymouth Sedan. But those who know say that it's a Ford.

Then he goes into the bar, where a denizen burns a hole in his chest with a cigar. But as the cigar is pulled away, the burn disappears for a brief moment before returning in the next shot.

A couple of errors even dog Linda Hamilton. As she runs down a hospital hallway barefoot, you hear the pitter-patter of feet wearing shoes. A little glitch from the Foley stage.

Later, she tells the doctor that there are 215 bones in the human body. He should have corrected her—there are only 206. Another thing about this sequence bothered many viewers—if she's in a high-security hospital, how could she get out with something as simple as a paper clip?

The film is plagued with examples of glass breaking out then popping right back in. One of the most obvious happens when Robert Patrick, as the "bad" Terminator, drives the heavy wrecker over the bridge into the Los Angeles River—yep, that's what it really is; that's the best we can do for a river out here!

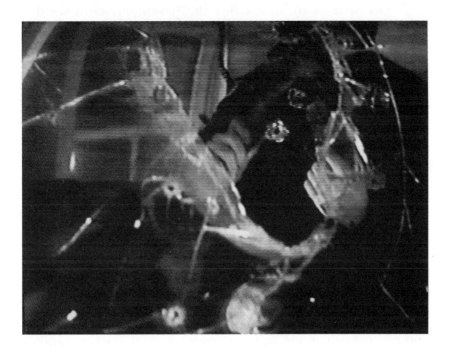

11

Notice that as the truck hits the pavement, both windshields pop out. But in the very next shot, as the chase continues, they're back in place, albeit cracked. The glass broken out of the guard shack at the hospital by Arnie also returns in a later shot, as does a rear window in the police van as they're being chased by a helicopter. And while we're at it, in a close-up you can see a hole blown in the helicopter's windshield. In a later long shot, the hole's gone.

When Schwarzenegger, as the "good" Terminator, and young Edward Furlong are in the parking lot and Furlong tells him to put the gun down, he does so on his right side. But when Furlong picks the gun up, it has moved closer to the other side.

When Robert Patrick transforms into Furlong's foster *mother*, he kills the foster *father* with his left arm that's been turned into a blade. But when he falls into the molten metal and "rewinds" through his various transformations, Patrick's right arm is the blade.

Speaking of the molten metal sequence, an electrician noted that when she lowers Arnold into the soup, Linda Hamilton pushes the button on the control panel that would normally raise him up rather than lower him. Was this a last-ditch rescue attempt?

We close with our favorite *T2* flub: look closely as Robert Patrick chases the police van in the helicopter. A couple of times when he's using both hands to reload his gun, you see an extra hand sneak out to fly the helicopter. We know he could transform himself, but an extra hand? It's surely the real-life helicopter pilot.

While we're at it, we have to report a few flubs from the first Terminator movie. We received several letters pointing out problems as the characters moved from one film to the next—young John Connor's ages, script logic, etc. However, we have to realize that these are fictional works, and trying to tie an original and a sequel together is putting just a bit too much reality into an unreal product.

However, in *The Terminator* (1984), a few funnies did pop up. For one, Linda Hamilton goes to a pay phone to call the police because she's being followed. She puts a quarter in and dials 911. She didn't have to do that; 911 calls do not require a coin deposit.

Schwarzenegger tries to locate Linda Hamilton's character, Sarah Connor, by looking up her name in the phone book. There are three Sarah Connors, with addresses beginning with 1823, 2816, and 309. Arnie tries to eliminate them methodically, but when he arrives at the home of the first one, it's 14239. Was there madness in his method?

When he walks into a police station looking for Sarah, he talks briefly to a cop, recites the famous "I'll be back" line, then leaves. The cop returns to his paperwork, then is caught in the glare of headlights as the Terminator's car crashes into the station. The cop is shown again, still in the headlights. But when the car crashes in, the headlights are off.

ROMAN SOLDIERS DON'T WEAR WATCHES

If there's ever a gremlin that's lurking around just waiting for a moment's inattention by a film costumer, it's the one that is in charge of watches and wedding rings. After all, the roles in historical or period films are being played by modern-day actors for whom wearing anything from Rolexes to Reeboks is such a routine, everyday thing that it's very easy for these items to go unnoticed.

It's Half Past Ten, M'Lady

Not to be outdone by the Greeks, a time-conscious character in the British-made *The Viking Queen* (1967) is clearly seen wearing a wristwatch.

Holy Moses

Perhaps the most egregious appearance of a watch in a historical movie happens in one of the greatest epics of them all—*The Ten Commandments* (1956)—when a blind man is seen wearing one on his wrist. Wonder if they made Braille timepieces back then?

The Revolt Begins at Nine O'Clock Sharp

In *Spartacus* (1960), it seems that some soldiers didn't want to be late for battle. Look closely. You'll see several wearing wristwatches. And some of them wanted to make sure that they'd be sure-footed in the heat of battle. You can see more than one soldier charging up a hill wearing tennis shoes.

Midair Collusions

Tom Cruise's wristwatch changes during the training flight in *Top Gun* (1986) from the one he had on when he boarded the plane. But then again, what can we expect since in the final battle the tail number on his plane changes several times in mid-flight?

Cape Fear

Cinema master Martin Scorsese is not immune from flubbing—even in a film as precisely and suspensefully assembled as *Cape Fear* (1991). Perhaps the most noticed flub in it happens when Ileanna Douglas and Robert De Niro chat in a bar. As she talks, the top button on her blouse is undone. Seconds later she buttons it, then it goes back to unbuttoned and buttoned without her ever touching it.

 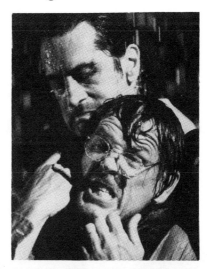

17

Later De Niro watches as Nick Nolte checks in at the airline ticket counter before boarding a plane. De Niro then asks the agent if Nolte is on the flight and when he is returning. Try that yourself and see what kind of response you get. According to a flub spotter in the know, airlines do not allow ticket agents to release this information. It takes a high-ranking official with proper security clearance to pull up a passenger list.

Young Juliette Lewis has a bit of a problem with the family vehicle. She says that she's grounded from driving the Jeep Cherokee as punishment for smoking. Unless somebody traded cars in the meanwhile, when the family flees they're in a Jeep Wagoneer. Small difference, but a goof nonetheless.

Another *Cape Fear* flub relates to Nick Nolte's statement that he had to go to hearings before the American Bar Association as a result of his criminal actions toward De Niro. We have this on high authority—no less than the Hon. Stanley M. Billingsley, of the 15th Judicial District of Kentucky. Judge Billingsley points out that the ABA doesn't license lawyers and has no authority to disbar them; it is a national lobbying association. Nolte would more properly have to go before the North Carolina Bar Association, given that Cape Fear is in that state.

TITLE TROUBLES

It's really tough when you find that you can't even trust the title of a movie. After all, the title is supposed to give you at least a vague idea of what to expect, isn't it?

If such is the case, why is it that in *Abbott and Costello Go to Mars* (1953) they don't ... they go to Venus? Or, if the title says *Abbott and Costello Meet the Killer, Boris Karloff* (1948), the often-evil Mr. K. is *not* the killer? Hmm.

In his delightful book, *Movie Clips* (Guinness Superlatives, 1989), Patrick Robertson also tells of the German film *Eine Nacht in London* (1934), which was released in Britain as *One Knight in London.* In the event that you're one of those who subscribe to Mark Twain's quote that "Life is too short to learn German," "Nacht" means "night." Dark knights are another matter entirely.

Robertson also tells us that the British *The Amorous Mr. Prawn* (1962) was about a general's wife who opens their official home to paying guests. However, in a display of unbelievable opportunism, the film was released in America as *The Playgirl and the War Minister,* notwithstanding that there was neither a playgirl nor a war minister in the film. It was, however, the year of the 1962 Profumo affair. Go figure.

Then, on the other hand, when the American Western *A Big Hand for the Little Lady* (1966) was released in Britain, it was retitled *Big Deal at Dodge City,* despite the fact that it took place not in Dodge City but in Laredo. (It was written initially for television as *Big Deal in Laredo*—at least *they* got it right.)

More titular tittering:

A Ruse by Any Other Name

What does a studio do when it has the misfortune of releasing a picture with the term "Communist" in the title just as Senator Joseph McCarthy was making it a truly dirty word? RKO simply changed the title of *I Married a Communist* (1950) to *Woman on Pier 13* in mid-run (in some locations it showed with one title, in others with a new one). Some filmgoers thought they were going to see a patriotic potboiler, while others presumed they would be viewing a "lady in distress" flick.

An A.K.C. A.K.A.

Not only was there not a character named "Lassie" in *Courage of Lassie* (1946), but also the gender-crossing collie played Elizabeth Taylor's dog "Bill." In opera, they'd call it a "pants role." In film, it's just a way to get the star's name in the title.

A MISHMASH OF MISMATCHES

The cut from one scene to another opens a wonderful world of mismatches—scenes that simply don't connect. Something might move. Time can accelerate. Things get fixed or unfixed. Actors move from place to place. Cars get traded. Food is replenished. Welcome to the mismatch mishmash:

A Bloody Little Gaffe

Just before young Indy (River Phoenix) receives his trademark fedora (in 1989's *Indiana Jones and the Last Crusade*), he gets roughed up and the dribbling blood on his chin switches from the left side to the right.

Maybe He Decided Not to Retire

Early in the horrific film *Seven* (1995), Morgan Freeman's character name, "Somerset," is partially scraped off his office door leaving "erset" as he prepares to retire from the force. But a shot later, the full name is back again.

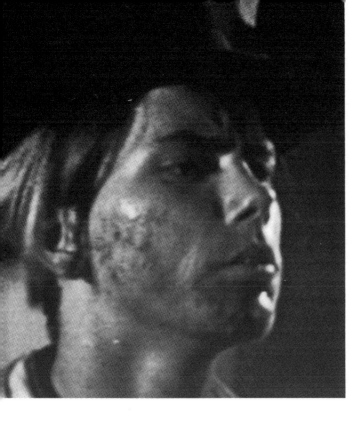

The Reincarnated Hamburger

We just can't leave Spielberg alone. At the beginning of *E.T.* (1982), Drew Barrymore and her mother (Dee Wallace) are eating dinner. Watch Drew's hamburger as it is restored from being half-eaten to whole, then it's gone. And when everyone's saying good-bye to E.T. at the end of the movie, in the background Mom stands up twice in less than a minute.

Jettisoned Jets

Smuggler Paul Bartel lands in New York in *The Usual Suspects* (1995) in a jet which, when seen from the front, has four engines. Cut to a rear view of the same landing plane and it has only two.

A Reversal of Fortune

Flipped film causes campaign signs in *Nixon* (1995) to read noxiN when Anthony Hopkins enters a ballroom at Los Angeles' Beverly Hilton hotel.

The Big Hand Is On The...

In a classroom scene in *My Life* (1993), the teacher tells the class that it's 2:30, but the clock on the wall behind her says that it's 2:55.

Not-So-Close Encounters

The Richard Dreyfuss and Teri Garr encounter is not so close when they approach Devil's Tower in Steven Spielberg's *Close Encounters of the Third Kind* (1977). The two see it for the first time when they climb over an embankment, but are stopped by the military as they approach the site. The problem is that they were closer to it the first time than when they're stopped. Notice, too, how the license plate on their station wagon changes several times as they break through the roadblocks.

The Nom-de-Steam Vanishes

In the 1938 version of *The Lady Vanishes*, dear old Dame May Whitty's Miss Froy writes her name on the steam-frosted train window. But a few shots later, the writing has moved to another place, and is entirely different. And, just to continue in the great tradition of continuity errors stretching across the years, in Cybill Shepherd's 1979 remake of the same film, her dress shoes magically become her trademark running shoes as she chases the train.

The Devil Made Me Do It

In *National Lampoon's Animal House* (1978), the word "Satan," which is written on a blackboard, looks totally different from one shot to another.

Shifting Ships

As the liner carrying the cast passes the Statue of Liberty in *The Last of Mrs. Cheyney* (1937), the name on its bow is "Rotterdam." When Robert Montgomery talks to the purser, it becomes the "Northhampton." Later, when Joan Crawford and Frank Morgan stroll on the deck, it's the "S. S. Britain."

Flashback Follies

Flashbacks are a real problem when you're going back from one film to another. A director has to be on his toes to make sure that that which is recalled is that which happened in the original. If not, someone is sure to catch it (see *Rocky* flubs). In *Superman II* (1980), the flashback to Jor-El's speech about the villains General Zod, Ursa, and Non is different than it was in the original. Another flashback flub is that Superman's mother (Susannah York) places him in the earthbound capsule; his father (Marlon Brando) did it in the original.

To Live and Die on the Freeway

There's many a Los Angeles driver who'd like to know how the owner of a brown van pulled off an amazing feat in *To Live and Die in L.A.* (1985). In one shot, you see the van hopelessly tied up in a freeway traffic jam. But seconds later, the same van comes driving by.

She'll Have Braids in an Hour or So

The baby in *Once Around* (1990) must have some amazing growth hormones. In the baptism scene, its hair grows from the time it is placed in Gena Rowland's arms to the time that Holly Hunter picks the child up and storms out of the room. We have to assume that this is because almost any scene involving an infant in a movie is filmed using twins or triplets. Screen Actors Guild and Child Welfare rules prohibit keeping a baby under the lights on a set for more than a very few minutes.

Saving the Stunt

Mel Gibson handcuffs himself to a man he tries to trick out of suicide in *Lethal Weapon* (1987). The man jumps anyway, and as Mel falls with him, if you slo-mo the video, you'll notice that the rubber trick handcuffs break, so they join hands to complete the illusion.

Heston Changes Planes...and Changes Planes...and

An aviation buff noted that the use of so much leftover footage from *Thirty Seconds Over Tokyo* (1944), vintage Japanese war films, and stock War Department footage created aviation magic in *Midway* (1976). Charlton Heston, as Captain Matt Garth, takes off to bomb the last Japanese carrier in a Grumman TBM Avenger torpedo bomber, flies along with his men in a Douglas TBD Devastator torpedo bomber, attacks the carrier Hiryku with a Douglas SBD dive bomber, and then crashes to his death in a Curtiss SB2C Helldiver dive bomber (which didn't go into service until a year after the battle). The film also uses the Chance Vought F4UK Corsair and Grumman F6F Hellcat fighters, which weren't in use until well after the Battle of Midway.

Level of a Whiskey

In a scene of *Scent of a Woman* (1992), Al Pacino and Chris O'Donnell argue as Pacino sits in a lounge chair and drinks from a glass of whiskey, the level of which continually rises and falls throughout their argument.

The Turning Point

In the opening scene of *Dave* (1992), the blades of the President's helicopter wind down and stop. In the next shot, the shadows show the blades still turning.

Mismatches Making Mismatches

The action comedy, *The Hard Way* (1991), features Michael J. Fox and James Woods as a mismatched duo—but their roles are nothing compared to the mismatches which show up on screen. Early in the movie, the sweat stains on the neck of Fox's T-shirt continually go from larger to smaller to larger to smaller.

When the pair has a set-to in a movie theater, Woods starts the fight with his last two fingers taped together. When he throws Fox into a popcorn machine, there's no tape; in fact, he opens his hand wide. Then the tape is back again—on his index finger. And when Fox loses a shoe during the climactic fight atop the cigarette billboard, it sure seems that the shoe is back on again as he dangles from the sign and maybe even again when he's on an ambulance stretcher.

Joe Pesci—Best Supported Actor

Entertainment Weekly found that Joe Pesci had to face up to a flub in *My Cousin Vinny* (1992). To smooth a few years off the actor's face, makeup artists used "lifts"—tiny pieces of netting, glued to the skin, then pulled back under a toupee—said one of their number, Carmen Willis. But the devices tended to slip, slide, and disconnect, causing several scenes to be reshot. But the magazine reports that even so, some of the tabs can be seen in the finished film.

That'll Take the Curl Right Out of Your Hair

You can make your own joke about this one—but why, in *Final Analysis* (1992), was Kim Basinger's hair curly when she jumped into the sack with Richard Gere and, as a *Los Angeles Times* reviewer pointed out, "straight as an ironing board" afterward?

Hair of the Duke: The Adventure Continues

We're back on John Wayne's hair again. We told you about the problem with his hairpiece in *North to Alaska* (1960) in *FILM FLUBS*. Now we've learned that in *The Quiet Man* (1952) when he fights with Victor McLaglen, he isn't wearing his rug. So when McLaglen's first punch knocks Wayne's hat off, we see much less hair than he has anywhere else in the film.

Engine Trouble

In *Always* (1989), when Holly Hunter bikes out to the airplane to say good-bye to Richard Dreyfuss, the right engine is shut down as she climbs up on the plane. Even though there was no opportunity to start it during the scene, when she climbs back down the engine's running.

Meet Me on the Porch Rail

Watch Judy Garland as she sits on a porch rail during the early part of *Meet Me in St. Louis* (1944). First she's sitting on the middle of the porch rail, then she's so close to the column that she can caress a rose, then she's back in the middle of the rail again.

Wet and Dry in Casablanca

Here we go—picking on *Casablanca* (1942) again. In a pouring rain, Rick (Humphrey Bogart) gets soaked while in a train station reading a note from Ilsa (Ingrid Bergman). In the next shot, when Sam hustles him onto the train, they're both perfectly dry.

Background Briefing

When William Petersen talks to his son in a grocery store in *Manhunter* (1986), they move down the aisles, then stop. Even though they're standing in the same place, carrying on the same conversation, somehow the background of canned goods changes as they talk.

They Felt Bad About It, So They Fixed It

The front yard is cluttered with junk, including a white chair swing hanging from one chain, when Ron Kovic (Tom Cruise) visits the family of the man he accidentally killed in Vietnam in *Born on the Fourth of July* (1989). But while he is in the house, someone must have slipped out and fixed the swing because it's hanging from both chains when he gets back into the cab to leave.

If This Doesn't Work, Drive a Stake Through Its Heart

Near the beginning of *Casino Royale* (1967), John Huston lights his cigar as a signal for mortar fire to destroy David Niven's mansion. The place blows sky high on the first hit—then in the next it's whole again, then destroyed again.

Wilting Ardor

Michelle Pfeiffer's mobster lover walks down the hall carrying a lavish bouquet of flowers in *Married to the Mob* (1988). When he arrives five seconds later, the bouquet has wilted to a skimpy business wrapped in white paper.

Make Up Your Mind, Katharine!

Paul Newman takes Katharine Ross for a bicycle ride during the "Raindrops Are Falling on My Head" number in *Butch Cassidy and the Sundance Kid* (1969). She comes out of the house and sits on the handlebars of the bike; but as they ride around they're in an orchard, with Ross sitting on the crossbar in front of Newman. Then as they leave the orchard, she's back up on the handlebars again.

A Window of Opportunity

A never-say-die situation also happens in *Die Hard* (1988). Terrorists bolt a missile launcher to the ground, shatter a window as they fire it, and destroy a police car. Bad guy Alan Rickman orders them to do it again, so they fire it through the same window, shattering it once more.

Sooner or Later He'll Get It Right

Patrick Swayze can't make up his mind about his coat in *Dirty Dancing* (1987). As he and Baby (Jennifer Grey) are about to dance at the end of the movie, he first starts to take off his coat in a long shot. Then in a close-up, he once more begins removing it.

Making a Clean Breast of It

Things get pretty interesting in *Fatal Attraction* (1987) when Michael Douglas is getting dressed after making love, leaving Glenn Close still in bed. From the foot of the bed, you see Glenn's exposed breasts, then there's a cut to a side angle where the covers are up to her neck. Then it's back to the foot where she's exposed again, then to the side where she'd once more covered.

And for a bit of marathon lovemaking, notice the clock when they're at it in the kitchen. They start at 4:45, and are still at it at 6:15.

A Call to Arms

After Jamie Lee Curtis shoots the killer in the leg and he limps away in *Blue Steel* (1990), you soon see him in her bathroom pulling the bullet out bare-handed, from his arm. And notice how many shots Jamie Lee can fire from her police revolver without reloading.

Mis-M*A*S*H

Boston film reviewer Nat Segaloff reports a series of confusing edits in Robert Altman's classic *M*A*S*H* (1970). First, there's the subplot about Ho-John, the mess-hall attendant who is filled with amphetamines by the 4077th medics to attempt to keep him out of the Korean military. He is dropped off at the examination center, and that's the (supposed) end of the sub-plot. Later, however Ho-John turns up as a war casualty in a brief scene. He's the "body" for which the doctors get blood by tapping into a sleeping Colonel Blake. Ho-John is lying on his side on the operating table before expiring and it's his body covered with a sheet atop a jeep behind where a poker game is later being played. The game is somber, and the camera arcs around it as the doctors stare out of the tent at the jeep. This, Segaloff says, explains the focus on the corpse in a film strewn with them. Ho-John is not just one more corpse, and footage explaining how he became a war casualty must be somewhere on the cutting room floor.

Another sequence shift comes when Major "Hot Lips" Houlihan (Sally Kellerman) arrives at the 4077th. Altman brought her in earlier and made her a major character in the film. But, if you look closely, when she gets off the helicopter, you can see Lt. "Dish" (Jo Ann Pflug) already in it. She is leaving as Hot Lips is arriving, although, since the continuity has been shifted around in the editing room, she has scenes still to come.

And...Segaloff alerts viewers to look at a scene showing the feet of the surgeons early in the operating room sequences. You can hear Elliott Gould's voice, even though his character is not introduced for another ten minutes.

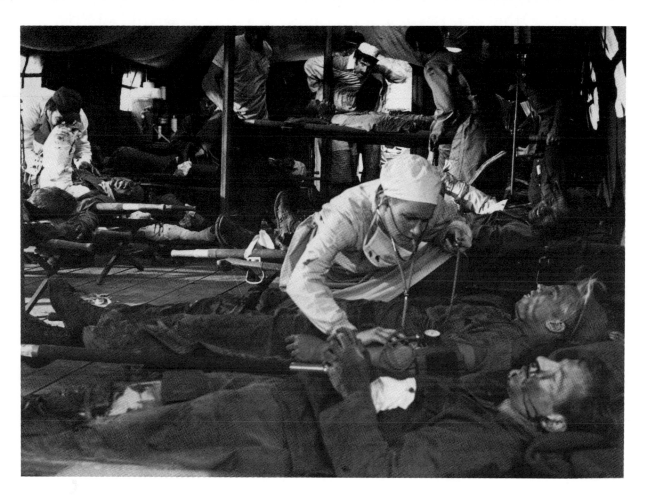

Forrest Gump

You don't have to be a mental giant to pick out the goofs in *Forrest Gump* (1994). You just have to be a sharp flub-spotter, especially one with a sense of history. Even though chronology played an important part in the film, a few slips of the calendar showed up. Well, flubs are like a box of chocolates...

Just before Tom Hanks, playing Gump, visits his wife's grave he says in a voice-over, "you died on a Saturday." However, when he visits her grave in the next scene, the tombstone shows the date of her death as March 22, 1982—which was a Monday.

In another scene, Robin Wright shows Hank a clipping in a scrapbook, under which is written "*USA Today*, 1978." *USA Today* began publication in 1982.

In a scene recreating the integration of the University of Alabama in 1963 a newscaster says "...here by videotape is the encounter..." TV stations didn't use videotape for news reporting in 1963; they used film.

When Hanks and Gary Sinese are fishing for shrimp, they pull in a Mello Yello soft drink can. It was established that the scene took place in the early 1970's, because Gerald Ford was President in a later scene. Mello Yello wasn't marketed until 1979.

And in an interesting background flub, watch the iron which rests on an ironing board in the background when Gump finds out he's a father. In the next few cuts, it's so surprised that it sits upright, then lies flat on the board, then returns to the upright.

IN THE TIME TUNNEL

For some of us, anachronisms are the most difficult thing to spot in a film; for others, the easiest. When something's out of its proper time frame, unless we have an expertise, the boo-boo passes on by, sans notice. But there's one thing you have to think of when you're making a film. Out there in the vast audience, there are always people who know their fields, whether it's music, art, automobiles, philately, whatever.

There are times when it's downright amazing. A philatelist noticed that in *The Two Jakes* (1990), a stamp on a letter that Jack Nicholson picks up came along about a year after the time of the movie. He could tell by the color of the stamp. Another noticed that one of the letters that Indy picks up in his father's study has a stamp on it that commemorates a hundred years of Texas statehood, one that was issued seven years *after* the time of the film.

A collector of Coca-Cola memorabilia pointed out that young George Bailey (later played by Jimmy Stewart) in *It's a Wonderful Life* (1946) works in a drugstore, and the narration indicates that he's "twelve years old in 1919." But he's standing next to a Coca-Cola thermometer—"the Silhouette Girl"—which wasn't produced until 1938.

Music is a real bugaboo. Those keen of ear and sharp of eye can always spot a song out of its time—whether (as pointed out in *FILM FLUBS*) it's "The Man That Got Away," crooned a mere twenty years before it was written by a saloon chanteuse to a young Lee in the 1988 *Liberace* TV mess of a movie, or other songs that were released not all that long after the movie's time frame—e.g., "Stop in the Name of Love," released in 1965 and "Reach Out (in the Name of Love)," released in 1966, in *Cooley High* (1975), which takes place in 1964.

Into the time tunnel:

What's Accuracy Got To Do With It?

A Marquee for a 1960 show features "Otis Redding, Martha and the Vandellas, Ike and Tina Turner" in *What's Love Got to Do With It* (1993). The Vandellas weren't formed until 1962, and Otis Redding wasn't playing as a solo act until 1963.

Stars and Stripes Forever

Throughout cinematic history, filmmakers have had problems in getting the proper American flag in their shots. Sometimes the prop person merely grabs the nearest flag, and doesn't count the stars. Other times, the current version of Old Glory may be flying on a nearby building. For example, there's such a scene in *The Godfather* (1972). It takes place in 1945, and you can see a 50-star flag. In 1945 there were only 48 states.

I Dub Thee Sir Johnson & Sir Johnson

Medieval King Arthur (Richard Harris), while expounding on the joys of his mythical kingdom, wears a band-aid on the back of his neck in *Camelot* (1967).

Nice to Meet You, Sir

Lionel Jeffries' character first meets King Arthur about an hour into *Camelot* (1967). But twenty minutes earlier, he is clearly visible at the King's wedding.

Aerial Errors

Mysterious Island, made in 1961, is set a hundred years earlier, in 1860. But when a hot air balloon rises into the sky, it emerges from a nest of television antennas.

And in *The Wrong Box* (1966), a similar problem arises—TV antennas are seen on the roofs of homes in England's Victorian era.

Precursor to a Disaster

At the beginning of *Wall Street* (1987), we're told that it begins in the winter of 1985. However, in an opening scene one stockbroker tells another that Gordon Gekko (Michael Douglas) was selling NASA shares ten minutes after the Challenger disaster—which took place in January 1986.

Tire Treads in the Sands of Time

The narrow wheels of the coach in John Ford's 1939 classic *Stagecoach* travel through wide tracks made by modern tires as they did in countless (mostly lower-budgeted) Westerns.

Long Time, No Funk

In a scene identified as "July 3, 1981," the young men in *Longtime Companion* (1990) dance to Sylvester's "Do You Want to Funk," a song that wasn't recorded until 1982.

The Christmas Conspiracy

We've uncovered some evidence that points to a conspiracy right within Oliver Stone's *JFK* (1991), evidence that could prove whatever we want it to prove (as some say the film did itself!). Seems that when Jim Garrison's fellow investigators are discussing Clay Shaw's use of the name "Clay Bertrand," they are sitting around Garrison's dining table, and there is a Christmas tree in the background. Garrison says he'll arrange a meeting with Shaw the following Sunday. That Sunday turns out to be Easter. Now...did he wait four months to set up the meeting with Shaw? Or did he create a clear and present danger in his own home by leaving a Christmas tree up for all that time, thus creating a fire hazard? Was it a "plant" (pun intended) to throw us off the trail? Perhaps we'll have to ask Oliver Stone to direct *Film Flubs: The Movie* to get the definitive answer.

Did It Take Him Four Years to Get Home?

A stamp collector noticed that in *Flying Leathernecks* (1951), coming home from the war, John Wayne takes a letter from a mailbox. In a full-screen shot, you can see a six-cent stamp—one that was issued in 1949, four years after the war ended.

It Was a Long, Long Speech

Early in *The Rocky Horror Picture Show* (1975), the narration says that the action takes place on an early November evening. In the next scene, as Barry Bostwick and Susan Sarandon drive through the rain, Nixon's resignation speech plays on the car radio. Nixon resigned and gave that speech in August...in the daytime.

We Have It on the Highest Authority...

We have an admission of a film flub from no less than Disney's Jeffrey Katzenberg, who responded to a reader query in *Premiere*. Reader John E. Silva noticed that the money used in *The Rocketeer* (1991) was deutschemarks. But the film is set in the 1930s, when Germany's currency was the reichsmark (used from 1925 to 1948). Katzenberg acknowledged and apologized for the error in the magazine's Gaffe Squad column.

Vampin' and Trampin'

In the 1979 television movie, *The Triangle Factory Fire Scandal*, the girls in the sweatshop, to break the tension during a rest period on the eve of the conflagration, decide to entertain one another by doing Charlie Chaplin imitations and dressing up as his famous "Little Tramp." The fire—and the setting of the movie—was in 1911. Chaplin was virtually unknown in this country until 1914.

Come Rain or Come Time

In a World War II sequence of *For the Boys* (1991), Bette Midler sings "Come Rain or Come Shine." But the song wasn't written until after the war and wasn't introduced until 1946, when it was part of the musical *St. Louis Woman*.

Strings of Time

We owe this one to a guitar enthusiast who noticed that in *Places in the Heart* (1984), the picker in a scene set in the 1920s is using a C. F. Martin "Dreadnought"—a guitar not yet invented at that time—and on closer inspection found that the instrument was fitted with Grover Tuners, which weren't marketed until the early 1960s. Our same sharp-eyed spotter noticed that in *The Godfather, Part II* (1974), when young Vito (Robert De Niro) sits on the stoop with his wife and children, a man behind them is playing a Gibson-style guitar that wouldn't be invented for at least thirty years.

Bugged by Bugsy

A time glitch in *Bugsy* (1991) bugged not only Der Flubmeister, but almost everyone we know who saw the movie. Near the end of the film, after Bugsy's own house has been sold to finance the Flamingo Club, he takes another look at his "screen test." He's at Virginia Hill's mansion, but he looks at the film in the projection room of his old house. Huh?

They Didn't Stay Within the Lines

Once again, the colorizers weren't paying attention. When *It's a Wonderful Life* (1946) was given the treatment, those who wield the evil computer paintbrush colored in the family photographs around the house. They didn't realize that the film was set in an era when color photography was rare and not really available to the general public.

47

Good Morning, World

A pivotal song in *Good Morning, Vietnam!* (1987) is "What a Wonderful World." The movie is set in 1965, but Louis Armstrong copyrighted the tune in 1967.

Welles Gets Wet

Orson Welles knew how to make a scene meaningful and moving, but he was all wet when in *Macbeth* (1948) he inserted one where King Duncan and his men renew their baptismal vows—led in a prayer composed by Pope Leo XIII in 1884. And think about this one: in *Marie Antoinette* (1938), viaticum is brought to the dying Louis XV (John Barrymore). The choir sings a Requiem Mass. Isn't that rushing things just a bit?

Grass Roots

Cher complains in *Mermaids* (1990) that Astroturf is going to ruin baseball. The movie takes place in 1963, and at the time artificial turf was still being developed under the trade name "Chemgrass." It wasn't until the carpeting of the Houston Astrodome in 1966 that the name "Astro-turf" emerged.

Misplaced Maple Leafs

Canadians noticed that the liquor crates in a warehouse raid in *The Untouchables* (1987), set in the 1930s, were printed with the stylized maple leaf symbol. However, the maple leaf didn't come into use as a logo in Canada until 1965, when the Maple Leaf flag was unfurled. In other films, Canadians laugh when they see the Royal Mounted Police on horseback. Despite the name, the Mounties appear on horseback only on ceremonial occasions. It's been years since they patrolled in the saddle.

Sneaking Into the Future

In Oliver Stone's *Born on the Fourth of July* (1989), one of the Vietnam-era vets is wearing Reebok sneakers in a scene set in 1972 at the Chicago Democratic Convention. Reeboks didn't come around until 1978.

Future Farmers

The Color Purple (1985) is set in 1938–39. One of the tractors on the farm has rubber tires, which weren't introduced to farming until 1945.

Flying Through a Time Warp

In filming the Japanese-American war epic, *Tora! Tora! Tora!* on Oahu in 1970, Japanese planes fly over KoleKole Pass, west of the Schofield Barracks en route to Pearl Harbor. In a rare irony, they fly right over a white cross memorializing the soldiers who were strafed by the Zeroes as they approached Pearl Harbor, the first casualties of the war. In the background you can see Tripler Army Hospital, built after the war in 1945.

Altered Time

Ken Russell's *Altered States* (1980) is set in 1967, but in the exterior shots you can see VW Rabbits, Plymouth Volares, and other 1970s cars.

The Prince of Tides

Before we get into it, there's something about this film we just have to discuss. What with all the controversy about Streisand's directing—which is, we have to admit, not bad—and the Oscar "snub," why would a director set up so many shots where the focus is on her star's (in this case, herself) glamorous manicure rather than on the scene itself? The constant display of nails is distracting, and we wonder if someone else had directed, would the show of hands been permitted?

51

We were also a bit troubled with Barbra's hands in one of the scenes in her office. As she sits on the front edge of her desk while talking to Nick Nolte, it seems that her hands make some awfully fast moves from her lap to the desk behind her.

The ever-so-sharp-eyed readers of *Premiere* magazine reported to our friend Rob Medich of the "Gaffe Squad" that when Nolte arrives at his sister's apartment in New York, he's in a Yellow Cab with the medallion number 6X24. Days later, he escorts Streisand's real-to-reel son, Jason Gould, to Grand Central Station, and the cab which takes them there once more is 6X24. And when Nolte and Streisand leave the disastrous dinner party, there's good old 6X24 waiting for them again. How's that for a cinematic coincidence, given that there are 11,787 licensed cabs in New York City?

When Susan Lowenstein (Streisand) takes Tom Wingo (Nolte) to her country home, they arrive laden with groceries. As they enter the house for the first time, almost all the doors and windows are open. Is it safe to leave your unoccupied place open in that part of the country?

You might also notice that while Nolte waits for Streisand across the street from her office building, there's a rather busy extra. A man in a light suit with shoulder-length blond hair passes behind him, right to left. Then, in a close-up, there he comes again, right to left.

SEASONAL SLIPUPS

'Tis the season...or 'tisn't it? Seems like "seasonal" blunders can appear from time to time in your favorite films, and usually there's an easy explanation. The season in which the film is shot is often far away from the one in which it is set.

Thus we're able to see the actor's breath in *In the Heat of the Night* (1967), even though the film is set in the hot, sultry Deep South.

Lawn Care

On the other hand, in the 1989 TV movie, *Cross of Fire*, the leading lady is encountered dutifully raking leaves on her front lawn, while all the trees are lush with green foliage—since filming was done in Kansas in mid-July.

This Is July?

In *Jaws* (1975), even though a picnic scene is set on the Fourth of July, the trees are winter-bare. (The scene was shot in May, before spring had completely sprung on Martha's Vineyard.)

A newscaster comments that it is "a nice spring day" in *The Day the Earth Stood Still* (1951). However, later in the film, it's revealed that the action takes place in July.

Pulp Fiction

Even those of us who aren't particularly attracted to the works of Quentin Tarentino couldn't help but like *Pulp Fiction*. Powerhouse performances by John Travolta and Samuel L. Jackson and one of the most original screenplay structures Hollywood has seen in a long time (even with the time-shift motif borrowed from Jim Jarmusch's *Mystery Train*) made *Pulp Fiction* one of 1994's most fascinating films. But it wasn't mistake-proof. For example:

One of the most fascinating flubs has to be rated "R," even in a book like this. Take a look at the first scene in the film, where Amanda Plummer yells, "Any one of you fucking pricks move and I'll execute every motherfucking last one of you!" Then, when the scene is replayed near the end of the film, she says: "Any one of you fucking pricks move and I'll execute you motherfuckers." Did they patch in a different take for the flashback? Hmmm…

Filmic technology gets the best of Tarentino in another replay scene. Most bullet holes are created by a "squib," a small explosive charge embedded in a wall or in a victim's clothing. In the flashback/expansion of the gun battle in the young men's apartment, a bullet hole appears in the wall behind Samuel L. Jackson *before* the victim begins firing at him.

Taking flubbery to the second power, gun afficionados noticed that when he kills the guy at the beginning of the movie, the slide on his gun is locked back in the open position, meaning that he's out of bullets. But, when the exact scene is replayed, the gun is loaded.

THE EDITOR GOOFED

The film may be in the can...but it often takes a brilliant editor to keep the entire movie out of the can. The work of this craftsman can be the difference between a great movie and a mediocre one.

Movies, as we all know, are shot in many short segments, called "takes," and the director and editor have to choose which ones show off the best performance or do the best job of moving the story along.

It's up to the editor to make sure the film flows seamlessly, and at the same time assemble it in such a fashion that it's visually interesting and involving, all the while taking the story to its conclusion. And a good editor can often find just the right shot or sequence to cover a director, cameraman, or actor's mistakes.

But what editor among us is perfect? A few cases in point:

Has Anybody Seen Old Whatshisname?

Steve McQueen stars as a bounty hunter in *Tom Horn* (1980). But perhaps there should have been a bounty on the head of the editor who spliced in one scene so that an actor got up from a table and instantly disappeared!

Backwards Thinking

Early in *Robocop* (1987), we see cars racing toward Dallas' famed Reunion Tower, the great golf ball in the sky. But when the shot changes to a reverse angle, the cars are speeding *away* from the tower, even though they have not changed direction. Something went wrong somewhere!

Backwards Thinking II (the Sequel)

Similar to the *Robocop* slipup, is the one when in *Carrie* (1976), director Brian de Palma had Sissy Spacek walk slowly backwards from a car in order to create the dream sequence car crash. Then the film was speeded up and run backwards to make it appear that the car was hitting Carrie. But another car accidentally got in the shot, and you can see it flash by, driving in reverse.

No Honors Here

Joe Pesci offers to carry Brendan Fraser's books in *With Honors* (1994), but in the next shot, they've inexplicably disappeared. But even more unusual is that later in the scene, flipped film causes "Harvard" to read backward on Pesci's sweatshirt and Fraser's cast to change legs.

Not the Greatest Edit on Earth

Several early shots in De Mille's *The Greatest Show on Earth* (1952) use the same background, edited in with the blue-screen matte process. When the editor cuts from shot to shot, the actors appear to be zapping back and forth, since there's no change in the size of the background.

The Other Side of the Window

When a movie is being shot on a soundstage, set designers sometime project background scenes onto the window frames to create the illusion of a real window. However, in *The Other Side of Midnight* (1977), someone goofed and switched the projection plates from one scene to another. First, you see mountains from a bedroom window. Then, in the next scene, you see the ocean in the very same window.

Robin Hood: Prince of Thieves

Rarely has a movie come along with such a disdain for historical veracity as *Robin Hood: Prince of Thieves* (1991). We touched on some of the errors in *SON OF FILM FLUBS*, but since so many more of the film's faults have come to light, it seems to be appropriate to devote a bit more space to a wry look at things which went awry.

To reiterate, the film is set in the 1100s. But when Azeem (Morgan Freeman) uses gunpowder, he's getting the jump on Marco Polo, who not only hadn't yet brought it back with him from China, but wasn't even born until 1254 and didn't make his famous journey until 1271. In the movie, the gunpowder was being used to defend King Richard, who died in 1199.

Azeem uses a crude telescope, predating both Dutch optician Hans Lippershey, who is credited with inventing the telescope in 1608, and Galileo, who built his first one in 1609

One apparent flub in the film may well be a matter of interpretation. Many viewers noticed that when we first see Azeem in the prison, his hands are chained above his head. When Robin (Kevin Costner) escapes, Azeem's hands are down and tied together. In the dark lighting of the scene it appears that Azeem has pulled away from the wall, stood up, and twisted the chains around his hands. Your call.

There's no question of a "left to right" flub when Azeem and Robin arrive on England's shores. Robin takes a celebratory roll in the surf, and then extends his right arm to Azeem for an assist in getting up. In the next shot, we see Azeem pulling him up by his left arm. Notice also how quickly the sand disappears from Costner's face after he kisses the surf/turf.

Poor Azeem. They just didn't seem to care about the veracity of his character at all. Another history buff noticed that throughout the film he carries a curved Saracen sword; if he indeed came from the Middle East, at that time in history the broadsword would have been the weapon of choice. The Saracen scimitar came along later.

In the river fight scene with Little John (Nick Brimble), Robin gets knocked into the drink several times. But his hair seems to go from wet in the close-ups to dry when we see him in the long shots.

We're not going to delve too deeply into the language situation in *Robin Hood*. Seems like every time we get into word usage, someone comes along with differing research that proves us wrong. However, it does seem that "twit" is a word way ahead of its era, and if the infamous "f" word was indeed in existence in the twelfth century, was Will Scarlett's (Christian Slater) "Fuck me, he made it" during the catapult scene a common usage of the time? (Webster's Ninth dates it back to around 1680). And of course, Costner's accent (or lack thereof) seems to originate more in Southern California than in Northern England.

Quintessential villain Alan Rickman, as the Sheriff of Nottingham, wears a heavy-metal costume enhanced with enough studs and buckles to make Michael Jackson jealous. Michael might also be envious of the codpiece, another element which seems to be ahead of its time. An ever-so-diligent viewer went to the *Encyclopedia Brittanica*, which said that the codpiece was "worn first in the fifteenth century," and wasn't "padded, prominent, and decorated" until the sixteenth. For those who aren't familiar with ancient costumery, a codpiece was used to make the male's crotch more prominent and decorative; "stuffed pants," if you will.

And speaking of that particular area of the body geography, another sharp-eyed viewer spotted bikini brief tan lines on Costner's buns. Are we talking eleventh century Speedos?

The slipups in *Robin Hood: Prince of Thieves* are not without historical precedent. In *The Adventures of Robin Hood* (1938), Errol Flynn jumps to his horse during a rescue scene with his hands tied behind his back. In midair, Flynn's hands are in front of him, then he lands with the hands once again tied behind his back.

And in an enterprising use of existing footage, during an escape scene in *Adventures of Don Juan* (1948), Errol Flynn and Alan Hale ride from the castle. The very next scene is a chase from their earlier *Robin Hood*, with bows and arrows and an extra head bobbing along on back.

We even have what you might call a "collateral" flub, coming from *The Rocketeer* (1991). There is a sequence in that film which supposedly takes place on the set of *The Adventures of Robin Hood*, wherein you see the back of a scenery flat from the Errol Flynn–Basil Rathbone duel. The problem is that a paper coffee cup with flap handles sits on one of the flat's crossbeams. The action may be taking place in the thirties; paper cups were, as best we can tell, a fifties product.

BACK FROM THE DEAD

Playing a dead body in an extended scene has to be a real challenge for an actor. After all, one does have to breathe from time to time. And blink. It's one of those involuntary reflex reactions to light, dust, or dryness which is very hard to control.

In the days of live television it was really a problem. There are several stories about "dead" actors getting up and walking off the set, not realizing that the camera was still on them. Movies, however, are another matter. The camera can be stopped to let the dead respirate. Even so, they can slip up.

Actors can experience a resurrection in other ways, too. Sometimes it's a matter of their being in a scene which becomes part of the story long after they've "died"—more often than not a result of nonsequential shooting.

Examples:

Depends on Your View of Reality

During one scene in *Total Recall* (1990), a psychiatrist is sent in to convince Arnold Schwarzenegger's character that everything going on is a dream. He says that he has been injected into the dream to bring him back to reality. Arnie responds by killing the doctor with a shot to the head. But later, when Schwarzenegger is being strapped down for reprogramming, the "dead" doctor is moving around in the background.

Dilating the Truth

We hate to break the illusion, but there are a couple of flaws in one of the greatest death scenes ever—Janet Leigh's departure in *Psycho* (1960). For one thing, she swallows after being dead. Neat trick. Then there's that extreme close-up of her eye. Notice that the pupil is contracted to a pinpoint, an obvious reaction to the bright lighting on the set.

When the movie was first released, director Alfred Hitchcock received letters from quite a few ophthalmologists, pointing out that when you're dead, your pupils dilate. They suggested that the effect could be created with belladonna eyedrops, which he used on the "dead" in later films.

Guttenberg's Movable Eyes

A young Steve Guttenberg, on the trail of Nazi-in-hiding Josef Mengele (Gregory Peck) in *The Boys From Brazil* (1978), is stabbed by Mengele's henchmen. He slumps to the floor with his back to the wall, supposedly dead. After which he blinks several times.

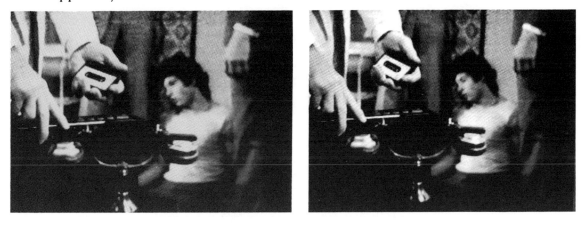

Just Keeping Up With What Was Going on in the Room

A dead man hangs from a coat hook behind a door in *Silent Rage* (1982), but as the door is slowly opened, the corpse's eyes move. When it's closed, they move again.

Politicians Never Die

The Vietnam vet holds a dead politician against a garbage truck in the Charlie Sheen–Emilio Estevez family epic, *Men At Work* (1991), while trying to convince the police officer that everything is okay. The corpse does its part; it blinks.

Speed

As *Speed* hurtled toward the big box office bucks in 1994, the fact that a bus could go more than 55 miles per hour during rush hour on the L. A. freeways wasn't the only thing that viewers found somewhat unbelievable about the action blockbuster.

Sharp-eyed viewers thought it was a bit unusual that even though Keanu Reeves shot Jeff Daniels in the left leg, when Daniels receives his police commendation, he's limping on the right.

When the bus made its famous special effects jump across the freeway gap, the poster on its side was loosened and dangled by a single bolt. But a few shots later as the bus heads down the runway at Los Angeles International Airport, the sign is back in place.

Just before the first bus explosion, Keanu takes out his keys to unlock his car door. Even though he never unlocks the door, after the explosion he opens the door and jumps right in. Guess we just never realized that an explosion which didn't damage a car could still activate a door lock!

69

One of the more interesting of *Speed*'s flubs involves Dennis Hopper, who is without a left thumb in the film. However, when he's holding the telephone in his right hand and talking to Reeves, we hear an audible snap of the fingers of his left hand. Pretty neat trick when you don't have a thumb.

And finally, Reeves calls his boss a lieutenant. But the film's credits say he's a captain.

THE FLUBS THAT COULD HAVE HAPPENED—BUT DIDN'T

A special niche in the world of flubdom has to be reserved for the ingenious filmmakers who knew that a flub was coming and managed to avoid it.

Epic director Cecil B. DeMille was a master of catching a flub aborning; in more than one instance he came up with some fascinating ways to keep the mistake from happening.

One near-miss was in *The Greatest Show on Earth* (1952). Gloria Grahame and Dorothy Lamour are in a carriage in the Marie Antoinette parade, wearing elaborate feathered headdresses. When the "dailies" came back, DeMille discovered that the film processing techniques in use at the time left a green tinge around the white feathers. So the clever DeMille inserted a shot of a light operator, high in the tent, aiming a green spotlight at the pair.

We have a group of Missouri Jesuit priests to thank for background on how DeMille was able to come up with a way to keep *King of Kings* (1927) true to biblical writ. Father William J. Federer reports that *FILM FLUBS* "entertained the Jesuit community here royally," and repays the favor by telling of the scene in *King of Kings*, wherein the woman "taken in adultery" is in the temple at Jerusalem, built for the movie as an elegant structure with a polished marbled floor. As told in the Gospel of John, Christ stooped to write on the ground as the woman was brought before him. Of course, that wouldn't have worked on the temple's marble floor.

So, to provide the dust, a girl enters carrying a bowl. She apparently hears a voice off screen summoning her, and runs away, tripping in the process. The bowl crashes to the floor, revealing that it was full of sand which spreads across the marble floor, giving Jesus a palette for his writing. An early Etch-A-Sketch, if you will. She picks up the pieces of the bowl and exits, and the scene proceeds as scripted in the Bible.

I hope the good fathers will forgive our retelling of a delightful *King of Kings* story, as related by Peter Hay in *Movie Anecdotes*. It seems that H. B. Warner, who played Jesus, took up with an extra named Sally Rand, later to become the famous "fan dancer." Rand played a slave girl to Mary Magdalene. One day, she and Warner arrived late on the set. DeMille thundered out through his megaphone: "Miss Rand, leave my Jesus Christ alone. If you must screw someone, screw Pontius Pilate!"

Softening the Way of the Cross

While we're at it, take a look at the scene in which Jeffrey Hunter as Jesus is carrying the cross in the 1961 version of *King of Kings*. He must have stopped off at the Jerusalem Plaza Mall on the way to the Via Dolorosa, because in a production still it sure looks to us like he's avoiding the pain of the cobblestones by wearing Hushpuppies. We thought sandals were the era's footwear.

Don't Fire That Guy...Reward Him!

Director Frank Capra knew when to take advantage of a flub. While filming a scene where a drunken Uncle Billy (Thomas Mitchell) staggers away in *It's a Wonderful Life* (1946), an offscreen technician bumped into a table full of props, knocking it over with a loud crash. The noise fit so well with Uncle Billy's exit that Capra left the serendipitous goof in the film and gave the guy a $10 bonus.

Incidentally, the above-mentioned H. B. Warner made a dramatic turnaround in *It's a Wonderful Life*, playing the town drunk.

Junk Food That Wasn't

Then another "flub that could have been" involves Meryl Streep's snack food in *Postcards From the Edge* (1990). Streep's character is a junk-food addict, going through bag after bag of Fritos Corn Chips. But several folks noticed that the chips she pulls out aren't Fritos. Nope, they're health food chips, which Streep asked propmaster C. J. Maguire to put in the bags.

Spooky Doings

In *Poltergeist* (1982), as writer David Hajdu notes, director Tobe Hooper had the actors walk up the steps backwards to create a supernatural effect, then reverse the film to obtain his spooky objective.

And he gleefully defuses the spectacular, glitzy effect when Esther Williams rises from the water with fiery sparklers in her headdress in *Neptune's Daughter* (1949). Run the tape backwards and you'll see that she was actually *lowered* into the water to create the effect, with the sparklers being snuffed as she went in.

Jurassic Park

It's hard to accept that a director who could make a film as magnificent as *Schindler's List* (1993) could flub up a film, but Stephen Speilberg's *Jurassic Park* (1993) had so many flubs that it turned up as the winner of the "Flubbic" Award as 1993's "Flubbed Up Movie of the Year."

One of the most obvious of the film's gaffes happens when Sir Richard Attenborough, playing Dr. Hammond, says "when they opened Disneyland in 1956, nothing worked." Disneyland actually opened July 17, 1955.

Other *Jurassic* gaffes (not counting all the plot lines which were left hanging for, we suppose, the sequel):

In the scene set at the archeological dig, an exterior shot shows Sam Neil entering a trailer whose door hinges are on the right. In the shot from the interior, the door hinges are on the left.

When Wayne Knight, playing computer whiz Dennis Nedry, steals the frozen embryos, the vial is labeled STEGASAURUS. The correct spelling is STEGOSAURUS.

Among other flubs spotted by super-observant *Film Flubs* readers are a previously dry jeep sprinkled with raindrops *before* the rain begins, an electric fan turning during a power outage, and visible special effects cables.

CREDIT CHECKS

The opening and closing credits of movies are rife with opportunities for the flub spotter with an eye for the awry. There's no telling what you'll find when you do your own credit check—misspellings, characters who weren't in the film but got a screen credit anyway, and all sorts of other surprises. Feast your eyes on some recently-unearthed favorites:

His First Credit

Director Beebe Kidron was pregnant during the filming of *To Wong Foo, Thanks For Everything, Julie Newmar* (1995). By the time the film was released the baby had been born—so in the end credits right after "Best Boy" there's a credit for "Best Baby...Noah Kidron."

The Enemy Within, the Enemy Without

The credits for *Public Enemy* (1931), that classic film in which James Cagney smashes a grapefruit into Mae Clarke's face, might well have left someone with a little egg on their own face. It turns out that while Louise Brooks is billed as "Bess" in the credits, she didn't appear anywhere in the film. Has anyone checked the famous cutting room floor?

Recalling the Error

When Disney's *Fantasia* (1940) was restored and rereleased in 1990, some of the early prints had to be recalled to correct a spelling error on Leopold Stokowski's name in the opening credits.

For the 'L' Of It

In *Total Recall* (1990), story credit is given to sci-fi novelist "Phillip K. Dick." It's "Philip," with one "L."

At Least It's Still Alliterative

Throughout the film, Melanie Griffith's character in *Pacific Heights* (1990) is called either "Patty Palmer" or "Patricia Palmer," yet in the closing credits, she's identified as "Patricia Parker."

Let's See…That's "I" Before "E" Except After "C," or Is It?

Sean Connery's character in *Outland* (1981) is spelled "O'Niel" on a computer screen in the movie, as well as in the end credits. But on his name tag, it's "O'Neil."

And She Made Such a Point of It, Too

Steve Martin's oh-so-L.A. girlfriend, Sarah Jessica Parker, in *L.A. Story* (1991) makes a big deal of the spelling of her name as "SanDee." Yet in the closing credits, it's "Sandy." Well, she tried.

From K to Z

Film and television maven Bart Andrews reports that in the classic *Casablanca* (1942), actor S. Z. "Cuddles" Sakall is identified in the credits as "S. K. Sakall." But Andrews, who reigns as one of the leading experts on television's "I Love Lucy," notes that even that classic show wasn't immune to a credit slip. Although Desi Arnaz was producer and co-star of the series, one season his closing credit read "Dezi."

More of the Name Game

The Hollywood Reporter columnist Robert Osborne has found that on the box for the videocassette release of *Demetrius and the Gladiators* (1954), Susan Hayward was identified as "Susan Hayworth." Someone must have gotten their redheads mixed up. But that certainly wasn't a first (or the last, we're sure). Osborne's *Daily Variety* competitor, Army Archerd, says that on screening cassettes of *Reversal of Fortune* sent to the Academy Award voters last year, Glenn Close's name was spelled "Glen" and director Barbet Schroeder's as "Shroeder."

Katharine Lost Her A's in the Deal

Hard as she tried over six decades of stardom, Katharine Hepburn had a devil of a time getting her name spelled correctly in the credits. It was Katherine Hepburn in *A Bill of Divorcement* (1932), just as it was again in *State of the Union* (1948).

And a Few Closing Comments...

Many a director likes to slip a few jokes into the closing credits. In *Ferris Bueller's Day Off* (1986), at the end of the credit crawl, Matthew Broderick reappears on the screen to ask, "Why are you still here? Go home!" or something to that effect. Several Burt Reynolds films show outtakes during the credit crawl, adding a bit of laughter to the list of names of people known, more often than not, only to their friends who worked on the picture and to their respective mothers.

The credits can even be provocative, as in *The Mission* (1986) where, if you'll wait until the end, you'll see the Bishop make a reappearance which seems to indicate that he's not at all sure of the correctness of his actions in the film.

End credit jokes can backfire, too. Outtakes showing Peter Sellers giggling and breaking character absolutely destroy the magic created just a few moments before in *Being There* (1979).

But the ZAZ team—Zucker/Abrahams/Zucker—takes the end credit spoofing to a new high. *Airplane!* (1980) lists "Author of *A Tale of Two Cities:* Charles Dickens" in its credits. In *Airplane II* (1982), right after the credit for "Best Boy," we get "Worst Boy: Adolph Hitler." In *Top Secret!* (1984), we see "Hey Diddle Diddle...The Cat and the Fiddle."

Ruthless People (1986) credits "Best Boy: Victor Perez" followed by "Best Pitcher: Dwight Gooden." In *The Naked Gun* (1988) there's "Dolly Grip: Jon Falkengren," "Poli-Grip: Martha Raye," "What the Hell Is a Grip? Person Responsible for Maintenance and Adjustment to Equipment on the Set."

Perhaps best of all are Abrahams's closing credits jokes in *Hot Shots!* (1991). Not only do you get a recipe for brownies and nobby buns, but there's also a list of suggestions for things to do after the movie, including "Help Someone Learn to Read" and "Visit a dairy and see how milk is handled and prepared for delivery."

At the end of the *Hot Shots!* credit crawl, you'll see "If you had left this theater when the credits began, you'd be home now."

And in *Lethal Weapon III*, if you wait out the credits, you'll see yet another building explosion and a possible setup for *LW IV*.

See what you missed?

The *Godfather* Series

Here we go again, into dangerous territory. Anytime you deal with movies as popular as Francis Ford Coppola's *Godfather* series, you're flying right in the face of some fans who've watched them carefully, time and again. But the same fans have found some interesting flubbery, even in the work of a master such as Coppola. Start the theme music...

In *The Godfather* (1972), when Michael (Al Pacino) shoots McCluskey the police chief (Sterling Hayden), and Tattaglia (Tony Giorgio), he fires at the chief's neck. McCluskey grabs his neck when the bullet hits, but in the long shot and the next close-up, the chief is bleeding from his forehead.

Also notice that at the toll booth massacre of Sonny (James Caan), the booth itself is properly aged and weathered, but a highway engineer noticed that the guard rail beside it is both new and of a modern design.

In *The Godfather Part II* (1974), as young Vito (Corleone) Andolini enters New York harbor on the ship *Moshulu*,

82

notice that the immigrants are standing on the side of the ship from which they would see the Statue of Liberty when they're leaving the harbor. The ship is actually going *downstream* past the Statue. That means that it's going out to sea, rather than into the harbor.

And in *The Godfather Part III* (1990), there's a problem with the papacy. The story is set in 1979, but Popes Paul VI and John Paul I figure prominently in the film; both died in 1978. In fact, a *New York Times* front page which carries an announcement of the appointment of John Paul I has a 1990 copyright date next to its March 27, 1980, publication date. Pope John Paul I was elected August 28, 1978.

OOPSIES

Some flubs defy explanation. They're usually just little slipups, things that nobody noticed on the set. By the time these oopsies make it to the final film, it's just too late to do anything about them.

Perhaps it's a little problem with a prop—such as in the controversial *Basic Instinct* (1992), where on the door plate of her office, the psychologist's name is spelled "Elisabeth Garner"; but when Michael Douglas pulls her name up on a computer, it's "Elizabeth Garner."

Then there's *Chicago Joe and the Showgirl* (1990), a British film. Remember that. British. The movie is set in London of the 1940s, and when Kiefer Sutherland is arrested by a Bobby, his rights are read to him. But the Miranda law didn't come about until the 1970s. Then again, why were they reading him his rights? Miranda is an *American* law.

More slips and slides:

Nothing Ever Is As You See It

Joan Blondell, turning up as Vi, the waitress in *Grease* (1978), consoles one of the students, who tells her, "Beauty school isn't what I thought it would be." Vi responds, "Nothing ever is," and heads into the kitchen with a tray of dishes. On the way in, she tries to flip off the light switch with her elbow and misses it by a country mile. The switch stays in the "on" position, but the lights go off anyway.

Privates Practice

A tickled and titillated viewer reports that in an episode of TV's *St. Elsewhere* wherein the doctors are in a steam bath, all are draped in towels. But when Dr. Morrison (David Morse) stands up, you get a quick glimpse of all his privates.

Wagner's Wingwang Wigwags

We'll take someone else's word for this one: in *All the Fine Young Cannibals* (1960), a film which we hear is so bad that one really just can't sit through it, Robert Wagner's wingwang can be seen to visibly wigwag through the fabric of his trousers. You go look. We don't wanna.

A Bit Too Flirtatious

One more, and we're off the subject (how's that for a double en-tendre?). In *Grease* (1978), when Dinah Manoff, playing Marty Mar-aschino, flirts with Edd "Kookie" Byrnes with the TV camera in the background, just after she says "Maraschino, like in cherries" her strapless dress slips, exposing a generous amount of breast. She quickly covers it with her dance card, but for a frame or two you can see her look of surprise. Kookie is out of frame at the moment, but we'd love to see the look on his face!

Shanghai'd From Shanghai

Exiled to Shanghai (1937) was not about anyone being exiled, and the story didn't take place in Shanghai. Then, in a case of film history repeating itself, no character, either male or female, is from Shanghai in *The Lady From Shanghai* (1948), Orson Welles's film that contains his famous Hall of Mirrors sequence. Welles said that he dreamed up the title to coax production money from studio boss Harry Cohn.

Best Breast Forward

Watch for this one on a late movie or one of the movie classics channels, since it isn't out on home video yet. In *Susan Hayward: Portrait of a Survivor*, a 1960 biography by Beverly Linet, Robert Wagner is quoted as saying that after hearing that a theater owner had spotted a delightful flub in *With a Song in My Heart* (1952), he couldn't find it. But never doubt the abilities of a dedicated flub-spotter. Martha Heneger says she found it in the title song number, about fifty-seven minutes into the film. The flub? Susan Hayward's strapless evening dress slips, exposing her left breast.

But Hayward wasn't the first to inadvertently be exposed on film. For a brief, one- or two-frame moment, when Fay Wray surfaces in the water in *King Kong* (1933), her dress slips and you glimpse a bit more of her decolletàge than either she or director Merian C. Cooper intended. And in *Red Headed Woman* (1932), a film that was made before the Hays Office did its dirty work, Jean Harlow briefly displays a breast.

Rodney Takes a Hairy Dive

Rodney Dangerfield takes a dive in *Back to School* (1986)—a "triple Lindy" from the high board. Look closely, and you'll see that it's Rodney starting the dive, but on the way down it's a double whose toupee flaps up to reveal his bald pate.

Anything to Help Out

When one of the hit men in the zany comedy *A Weekend at Bernie's* (1989) was knocked cold and dragged into a closet, he conveniently lifts his feet so the closet door can shut.

Going Off With the Bushes...But Not George and Barbara

You usually don't see too many flubs in animation, it being a meticulous, detailed art. But they do happen—as in Disney masterpiece *Fantasia* (1940). Notice that during the Pastoral Symphony sequence, when a pair of centaurs go off to woo, a bush at the bottom right corner of the screen goes along with them.

Take a Seat, Please

During the "Grant Avenue" musical number in *Flower Drum Song* (1961), dancers on the front row kick their feet forward and down on one hand, except for one who lands on her tushie.

2A or Not 2D

In *Soap Dish* (1991), when Sally Field asks the doorman the number of Kevin Kline's apartment, she is told "2D." But later, when she leaves, the number on the door is "2A."

Producer Alan Greisman admitted to an interviewer that it was an error caused by writing down the wrong numbers when the prop people went to buy them. It was noticed in edit and an attempt was made to re-record the doorman's lines to "2A," but this looked so awkward that the decision was made to leave in the gaffe.

Apollo 13

We really hate to pick on *Apollo 13* (1995), given that a close friend of many years had a large role in the film (yep, I remember when Chris Ellis, who played Deke Slayton,was an acolyte at my church). However, since no less of a venerable venue than *The New York Times* felt compelled to point out the movie's mistakes as discovered by NASA nabobs and scientists, look for these glitches:

The paint pattern for Saturn V is inaccurate, given that all of the Saturns which actually flew had black and white vertical stripes topped with a ring of black. The movie version uses the stripes without the ring.

When the astronauts are climbing into their space suits, you can see NASA's "worm" logo, which wasn't used until 1976. In 1970, the time of their flight, the NASA logo was stars and a "swoosh."

The engines were started a little late in the film. In a real launch, they would have been started at "T minus 9" rather than "T minus zero" as it was in the film. The hold-down bolts are released at zero.

The ship's gantry arms fall away in unison during a regular launch, not one at a time as they do in the film.

The sudden jolt when the first stage rocket separates was unexpected, not a normal event as portrayed in the film. Actually, Jim Lovell scratched his helmet when he banged into the switch guards.

The moon changes phase several times during the four-day journey of Apollo 13, when in actuality there was only one phase, a waning half moon which would give the astronauts the opportunity to land at sunrise. The long shadows would aid with navigation.

Another out-of-phase flub happens when the astronauts lose communication with the earth and simultaneously enter darkness on the back side of the moon. That's an event that happens only once every 28 days, and this wasn't the day.

An engineer uses a slide rule to double-check Tom Hanks's arithmetic. Hanks used addition and subtraction to calculate the capsule's angle of orientation—and slide rules aren't normally used for addition and subtraction.

If you take the evidence of one shot, the Apollo spacecraft would be as big as Australia. That's the result of the proportions in the shot where you see the sun, the moon, and the spacecraft.

A geographic gaffe happens when the astronauts point out the Sea of Tranquility. The shot you see is actually Hadley's Rille, landing site of Apollo 15.

Another impossibility is the shot of a full moon out of one window of the capsule as it's on its way back to earth, followed by a full earth on the other side. That would be possible only if the sun were between the moon and the earth, making us pretty warm. It might happen if the spacecraft was somewhere near Venus, which it wasn't.

Here's one that it takes a sharp mind to catch: In one scene, the ship is said to be rotating at 2.5 degrees per second; but the view out the window shows the earth passing by at about five times that rate.

And finally, in a scene whose point of view is outside the capsule you hear the roar of the propulsion jets. They wouldn't make a sound in the vacuum of space, unless you were right next to them, burning to a crisp.

We have to confess that it takes a particular eye for detail to catch the gaffes in what was otherwise a fine movie—but then again, that's what we expect of rocket scientists, isn't it?

FOLEY FOOLISHNESS

When he decided to go into the sound effects branch of the movie business, Universal's Ed Foley turned out to be such a pioneer that he joined the ranks of Kilroy, Murphy, Sandwich, Volt, Ampere, Boycott, Diesel, Bloomer, Crapper, and all the other worthies whose family name has gone into the language—on one hand immortalizing them, on the other stripping them of their status as real life human beings.

Foley gave his name to sound effects recording, and these days you see Foley editor, Foley artist, and Foley stages listed the in the credits of most films.

Foley work is part of the "sweetening" process. Often, the actual sound that's recorded isn't the one our ears are trained to hear, or isn't sufficient to carry the moment in the film. We're so ear-trained by the movies that the "real" sound of a thunderstorm doesn't register as well as a soundman's artificial thunder sheet. Likewise with a fight—the real-life sound of punching and smacking differs from what we hear on screen, whereas the onscreen sound seems like reality.

I recall reading that in *Apocalypse Now* (1979) the actual noise of the helicopters didn't sound right on the track, so it was replaced with an effect created by some chains in a paper bag. Of course, the most frightening sound in that movie, Wagner's *Ride of the Valkyries*, which heralded the silent approach of the helicopters, was produced without Foley devices.

The Foley artist reaches into his bag of cinematic tricks to create all kinds of noises—airplane engines, horse hoofbeats, footsteps, wind-storms, car crashes, etc.

For example: take breaking glass. On the set, any glass that breaks is probably going to be what the special effects artists call "candy glass," once made from melted sugar. When an actor goes through a prop window, it will not make too much noise—until the Foley editor puts it onto the sound track.

Similarly, in a fight scene, it's a rare actor who wants to take an actual punch (and a rarer insurance company that will allow it). As a result, the camera is set up so that the actors can aim a punch and score a near miss, with the air space eliminated by the camera's depth of field. The corresponding "thud" probably comes from a Foley artist slugging a rump roast or some similar material for the soundtrack. Most of the time you don't know the difference. But, if you're one of the flub spotters who noticed, in *The Godfather* (1972), that even though one punch misses its intended recipient by a country mile, the thud is there anyway.

As much as they enhance the workings of a film, there are times when the Foley work goes awry. For example: When a car roars off and/or spins out on a dirt road, we hear the tires screeching. On a dirt road? Come on! More cases:

Technical Trip-Up

Near the end of *The Firm* (1993), Tom Cruise rushes to print out some documents from his computer. At one point the screen says that the laser printer is printing, but the sound is the screech of a dot-matrix.

Hi, Judy, Judy, Judy

There's considerable debate about what might be a vocal gaffe in the famous "Trolley Song" in *Meet Me in St. Louis* (1944). During one of the verses, it appears that someone, thinking it was just a rehearsal, stopped by the set and said "Hi, Judy!"—and the greeting slipped by and went onto the final track. Liza Minnelli owned up to the story during a PBS tribute to her father, director Vincente Minnelli. But some folks say that it's "Hi ya, Johnny," rhythmically placed to greet John Truett (Tom Drake), the boy next door. Listen, and decide for yourself.

Meanwhile, Back in the Jungle

Remember that familiar, atmospheric "brrr-hoo-hoo-ha-ha" you hear as an establishing sound in just about every jungle movie you've ever seen, no matter if the setting is in Africa, South America, Asia, or a tropical island? Well, it's a ringer—the cry is that of the Australian Kookaburra, a kingfisher that lives only in the Outback and nowhere else on earth, except perhaps in a zoo or in a sound editor's bag of tricks.

The Case of the Subway Sex Change

USA Today film writer Susan Wloszczyna tells us that when she watched *Frankie and Johnny* (1991), she noticed that in a subway scene, a woman is on screen, but the voice we hear is that of a man. Hmmm...

Eat Your Heart Out, Milli Vanilli

When Michael Paré sings "On the Dark Side" in *Eddie and the Cruisers* (1983), he closes his mouth before his vocal solo ends.

No, Val, It's Jim They Want

Val Kilmer plays Jim Morrison in *The Doors* (1991). Near the end of the film, when he's in the shower with his girlfriend, the crowd is calling for him. She says, "It's you they want, Val."

A Well-Mannered Child

At the end of *Operation Petticoat* (1959), Cary Grant disembarks from the submarine and is met by Dina Merrill, along with a small boy and girl. The little boy says, "Hello, Mr. Grant."

The Writer Stands Accused

One has to wonder what kind of lawyer is defending Jodie Foster in *The Accused* (1988). When she is on the witness stand recalling her rape, he calls one of the men who raped her "the assaulter." Any law school graduate would have used "the assailant."

No, No, Douglas

Michael Douglas makes an emphatic point with Danny DeVito in *War of the Roses* (1989). As they look at house plans spread out on a desk, Douglas looks up and says, "No, no, DeVito!"

Lighten Up, Sly

When his pal Paulie (Burt Young) makes some disparaging comments about young boxer Tommy Gunn (Tommy Morrison) in *Rocky V* (1990), Rocky (Sylvester Stallone) responds, "Lighten up, Burt."

The Way We Almost Were

An editing cut near the end of *The Way We Were* (1973) has Robert Redford saying "ab awesome." Did an editor drop the "solutely"?

Foley to the Second Power

What we have here is a Foley/Foley situation. When Eddie Murphy, as
Axel Foley, goes to the gun club in *Beverly Hills Cop II* (1987), he watches
the "six-foot blond" (Brigitte Nielsen) using the firing range for target

shooting with a pistol. However, each time the gun fires, you hear a
"blam, tinkle, tinkle," indicating that her spent cartridges are falling to
the floor. From a pistol?

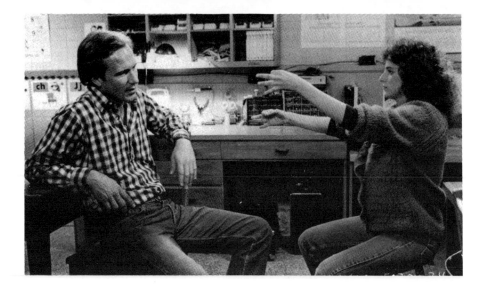

Dirty Hands

And while we're at it, what was going on in *Walker* (1988) to cause Marlee Matlin to sign "Fuck off"? We didn't catch it, but an alert gaffe spotter who could read sign language did. And another reports that in *Children of a Lesser God* (1986), filmed while Matlin and William Hurt were real-life lovers, there are times that the sign language conversation is not about the plot of the film, but idle chatter between the two about things going on in their offscreen life.

The Not-So-Silent Scream

Christopher Reeve bursts in on Michael Caine and Dyan Cannon in their bedroom in *Deathtrap* (1982) and Cannon screams. She screams so long, in fact, that when they go to a three-shot, she's still screaming even though her mouth is closed.

An Attack of English Amidst the Din

In the 1939 classic *Gunga Din*, the natives, none of whom speak English, are fighting. Yet within all the noise of battle, you can hear one of them yell "watch out" in perfect English.

An Impertinent Usher

Oh, no. We're back on the case of *Pretty Woman* (1990), winner of our first "Flubbie" for its plethora of gaffes. Now we find another: When Richard Gere and Julia Roberts are at the opera, the usher asks: "Will there be anything else, sir?" Gere says no, and the usher says, "the glasses are there, Julia." Julia's character was named Vivian.

Dial M for Mistake

Flub-spotter Stephen Ryan noticed that in Alfred Hitchcock's *Dial M for Murder* (1954), Margo Wendice (played by Grace Kelly) and Mark Halliday (played by Robert "Bob" Cummings) are having an affair behind her husband's back. In the opening scene, Margo reveals to Mark that someone is blackmailing her. Mark suggests that they should admit their guilt to her husband. Perhaps because she was caught up in the moment (or maybe she identified too strongly with her character), Grace addresses Cummings not by his character's name, but by his own, blurting out, "No Bob, please, you mustn't!"

Home Alone

We are troubled. We are greatly troubled. We are bothered that a simple little movie called *Home Alone* (1990) has become, as of this writing, the fourth largest-grossing movie in cinematic history. It's a pleasant time-passer with a cute kid and some funny bad guys—essentially a live-action version of a Road Runner/Wile E. Coyote cartoon. But up there in the stratosphere with *E.T., Gone With the Wind,* and the others? Wow. We despair as to what it says about today's audiences.

That being said, you can understand that we take particular delight in issuing a few jabs:

When pint-sized Macauley Culkin's mom (Catherine O'Hara) is frantically trying to get back from Orly Airport in Paris, it's obvious that the scene was filmed in another airport (apparently O'Hare in Chicago). You can see the tail of an Eastern Airlines DC-9 is in the background. Eastern doesn't fly to Paris (in fact, it doesn't fly at all anymore), but if it did, it wouldn't be in a DC-9, a short-range aircraft designed for domestic use.

Also when Mom leaves Paris, she departs on a American Airlines 767, and arrives on an American 757. Did she change planes along the way?

When the kid goes to the grocery, he buys Tide detergent among his other provisions. But at the end of the film, when he tells his mom exactly what he bought, he says that he bought fabric softener. He didn't.

And the wonderful Joe Pesci has a real problem with the hot doorknob. He grabs it with his right hand, then clutches his left hand with his right in pain, then he plunges the right hand into the snow. When he looks at the burned hand, the initial burned into it is upside down in relation to the way he grabbed the knob.

ILL LOGIC

In just about every interview we've done—and there have been literally hundreds—one question pops up time and again: "What's your favorite film flub?" That's like asking which is your favorite child—we love 'em all. But if there is a particular *type* of flub that we enjoy the most, it would have to be those that we categorize as "Ill Logic." These are the flubs that happen when the thought processes go slightly awry. Someone doesn't think about what they are saying, doing, or writing into the script; or artistic license is taken a bit to the other side of our suspension of disbelief.

For instance:

Night for Day

In *The Bodyguard* (1992), Kevin Costner and Whitney Houston arrive at the Academy Awards at night. The Academy Awards begin at 6 P.M. in Los Angeles (with celebrity arrivals in mid-afternoon) when there's still plenty of daylight. And in the same film, a mock copy of the *Hollywood Reporter* newspaper announces the Oscar nomination for Whitney Houston's character on the same page as the ratings for Game One of the World Series. The Academy Award nominations are announced in February, months before the World Series in the Fall.

Reflect on This

Risking the wrath of the Trekkies (or, as they prefer to be called, the Trekkers), it must be pointed out that in *Star Trek—The Motion Picture* (1979), when the *Starship Enterprise* flies past Jupiter and its moons, the light comes in at such an angle that there's a half moon, a crescent, and a full moon. Moons are, after all, reflective bodies and the implication is that the light comes from several different sources in differing directions.

We Know He's Strong, But...

At different times in *Junior* (1994) both Arnold Schwarzenegger and Emma Thompson pick up a vial containing an egg from a liquid nitrogen container—each time with their bare hands. In real life the container would freeze the skin on their fingers. Containers are usually removed from nitrogen with heavy gloves and tongs.

Man of Steel

Even though Christian Slater shoots John Travolta in the right arm in *Broken Arrow* (1996), a few scenes later Travolta has no problem shooting down a helicopter, arming a nuclear weapon, and fighting Slater with that same wounded arm.

The Psychic Identification

Holly Hunter shows a bit of psychic ability in *The Firm* (1993) when she positively identifies Gary Busey's killers. She was in the office when he was shot, but was hiding under his desk and could not possibly see them.

Don't Tell Universal

Fred Flintstone responds to a question in the affirmative in *The Flintstones* (1994) saying, "Is the world flat?" He must not have been looking at the screen earlier at the drive-in when the film opened with Universal's familiar round-earth logo.

The Naked Truth

One of the best slips of movie logic takes place when Claude Rains, in the elusive title role of *The Invisible Man* (1933), uses his invisibility to elude the police near the end of the film. He strips completely naked, head to toe. But take a look at the footprints in the snow that the police follow as they track him. They're made by feet wearing shoes!

Feats of Navigation

Lee Remick and George Segal pull off a rather amazing feat in *No Way to Treat a Lady* (1988). As they travel down the river in a police launch, they pass the Queen Mary twice, even though the launch never turns around.

Where Does Real Stop and Surreal Begin?

In the last quarter of *Barton Fink* (1991), John Goodman tells John Turturro (as Fink) that he is leaving the hotel and doesn't know when he will return. Goodman takes two suitcases, says good-bye, and walks out. A day or two passes, and in the middle of typing a screenplay, Turturro opens the door and places his shoes in the hall for shining. Goodman's shoes are in front of the door to the room that he keeps permanently, even though he's gone.

Shedding a Little Light on the Subject

The electricity is off in a scene in *White Palace* (1990). So why does the light come on in the refrigerator when the door is opened? Hmmm...

We've Never Had a Housekeeper This Fast

In the final moments of *The Time Machine* (1960), the housekeeper, who is alone in the house, closes the door after a departing Alan Young. Then we see both upstairs and downstairs lights go out in a matter of seconds. Did she zoom up the stairs, or did the house have a master switch?

A Modest Oprah

Oprah Winfrey is knocked out cold when pistol-whipped with the butt of a revolver in *The Color Purple* (1985). But when the wind blows up her skirt, the unconscious Oprah reaches out and pushes it back down.

A Not So Crystal Clear Case of Genetic Engineering

Now here's something to ponder concerning the "cow" that gives birth to the calf in *City Slickers* (1991). If Billy Crystal actually helped at the calving, he may well have been part of an event that made a bit of genetic history. Several farm-belt flub spotters will swear 'til the cows come home that the "mother" is a mixed-breed beef cow giving birth to a pure-bred Jersey dairy calf. It's a cinematic improbability and a genetic impossibility.

The Kid Needs Sleep Therapy

When Michael Douglas tucks his daughter into bed for the night in *Fatal Attraction* (1987), he looks out the window. It's dark, but you can see that his watch reads about 3:15. It's either a very dreary day or the kid is going to bed at a really strange hour.

The little girl also does some high-speed aging. At one point in the movie Anne Archer says that the youngster is five years old; but later, when Glenn Close asks Michael Douglas he says that she's six. There certainly hadn't been enough time for her to age a year. Or did she have a birthday party and we weren't invited?

A Few More Months and She Could Have Birthed an Elephant

A critic once pointed out that if you time Melanie's pregnancy to the Civil War battles in *Gone With the Wind* (1939), she was pregnant for twenty-one months. Informed of the time discrepancy, author Margaret Mitchell once replied that Southerners always do things at a slower pace than Yankees.

A Precursor of Things to Come

Here's another "point to ponder": in *The Ten Commandments* (1956), in a scene before the birth of Moses, an early Pharaoh decrees the slaughter of the Hebrew boys, announcing, "So says Ramses the First." Since the second didn't come along until about forty years later, shouldn't he have said "So says Ramses" and leave it at that?

Springtime in January

In the opening credit sequence of *Born on the Fourth of July* (1989), a young Ron Kovic runs home on a sunny day. There are leaves on the trees, and the kids are dressed casually. When he gets home, he sits with the family and watches John F. Kennedy's inaugural speech on TV. Since that happened on January 20, 1961, and the family lives on Long Island, shouldn't the trees be bare and perhaps some snow on the ground? Or was it just a very, mild winter?

And Then He Went Off to the Confederate Air Force

John Wayne, playing Ethan Edwards, returns home in *The Searchers* (1956), visits his brother's family, and gives his niece a medal which was given to him by the Confederate government. Superpatriot Wayne must have coined it himself; the Confederates didn't give medals.

Stopping Planetary Time

A considerable amount of time goes by while the extraterrestrial is hiding in a shed in *E.T.* (1982), but the moon never moves.

Is a Bird Bath the Fountain of Youth?

The story of *Birdy* (1984) is told in flashbacks which alternate between two G.I.'s (Matthew Modine and Nicolas Cage) who are in their early twenties in 1972 but are sixteen-year-olds in the 1950s—indicating that they have aged only about four or five years over a course of seventeen or eighteen. What are they eating?

 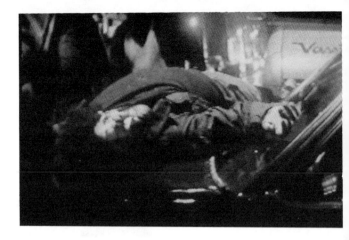

The Moving Dead

When Rick Aviles, playing a bad guy in *Ghost* (1990), is hit by a car and killed, notice that his dead body is lying on the street next to the car wheel as his spirit emerges. But when the spirit takes a disbelieving look at his corpse, it has moved upward and is on the hood.

Presumed to Be Recording

Having once interviewed two of Hollywood's top producers with dead batteries in my tape recorder, your humble scribe can certainly sympathize with the reporter who thrusts a tape recorder in Harrison Ford's face as he leaves the courthouse in *Presumed Innocent* (1990). You can see that there's no cassette in it; the recorder is empty.

Another Angle on Eastwood

In the scene about Clint Eastwood's "rape" in *The Rookie* (1990), a video was shot with the camera facing Eastwood. There is only one camera and it's turned on and left running. Thus all the shots should be from the same angle. But when the video is played back it's from several different angles.

Love Means Never Having to Say It Makes Sense

Love Story (1970) is a relatively simplistic tale, offering little to think about. But consider this: Jenny (Ali MacGraw) and Oliver (Ryan O'Neal) are at a skating rink when she tells him she's ready to go to the hospital. They trudge up a snowy hill and at the top they hail a cab for the trip. Later, after Jenny dies, Oliver walks out of the hospital, crosses the street, and walks down the hill to the same skating rink. If the hospital was right across the street, why did they take a cab earlier?

Sorry, Wrong Number

Tony Randall phones Doris Day from Rock Hudson's telephone in *Pillow Talk* (1959), getting a busy signal. But the plot line of the movie is based on the fact that Rock and Doris are on a party line. And in the 1989 TV remake of *Sorry, Wrong Number* with Loni Anderson, why does her husband call her person-to-person from a phone booth (to establish an alibi) when he knows she's bedridden and alone in their house?

A Cop Car the Crooks Would Love

In *Another 48 HRS* (1990), Eddie Murphy and Nick Nolte sit in the back of a police car talking to a man. They finish the conversation and then open the rear doors to get out. Think about it. A police car, with rear doors that open from the inside. The bad guys love it.

Selective Grunge

Jack Nickolson's face is eaten by a grungy substance in *Batman* (1989). But it doesn't bother his deck of cards—paper being tougher than skin, we suppose.

Wendy and the Wind

It's a stormy night in Scotland when Wendy Hiller, a headstrong young lady on her way to marry a very rich man, is forced to stay over in a coastal house in *I Know Where I'm Going* (1945). The storm makes passage to the island impossible. She paces around the room while it rages outside. Inside the curtains blow even though the windows are closed. What a drafty house!

Sure ... You Try It

Knowledgeable audiences laughed in *No Way Out* (1987) when a character says that it will take twenty-four hours to check every corridor in the Pentagon. It would take days, maybe. Probably weeks.

Star Trek

Perhaps we should don a suit of armor. We're going to talk about a series of films with devotees who know them frame by frame. Stand back—we're going to talk about the *Star Trek* movies.

Elsewhere, you'll find some notation of flubs in the *Star Trek* TV series. There is, of course, a bit of crossover between the two, one instance of which produced a TV-to-film flub (see page 139). However, since we're dealing with film here, we'll keep them separate.

We have quite a few Trekkies (or is it Trekkers? We've heard that one term is acceptable, one isn't, so forgive us if we err) who were more than happy to share their favorites. Beam us up, Scotty.

In *Star Trek—The Motion Picture* (1979), there's a scene where Spock is floating around outside the Enterprise. Kirk has discovered that Spock is gone, and leaves the ship through an airlock. The close-ups show Kirk floating away from the ship, then in the next shot, if you look carefully you can see the ceiling of the soundstage, with interior stage walls to the right and left. The camera has pulled back too far.

In *Star Trek II: The Wrath of Khan* (1982), when told that Spock is dying, Kirk runs to the engine room with his jacket buttoned all the way up. But when he reaches the engine room, it's opened all the way back with the white flaps showing. Then when he gets to the glass, one lapel shows with the red side of the other jacket buttoned across it. When he slides to the floor, both white jacket flaps show again.

Also notice that Kirk is given a pair of antique glasses, later dated in *Star Trek IV* to be from the eighteenth century. But the ear pieces are modern clear plastic.

In *Star Trek IV: The Voyage Home* (1986), watch a young nun standing by the aquarium as she inexplicably changes into an older nun. Also, in the scene were Sulu pilots a helicopter carrying a large crate, watch the changing position of the plastic between the time he flies toward San Francisco and lowers it onto the Klingon ship.

And finally, in *Star Trek V: The Final Frontier* (1989), watch the changing colors of Shatner's tunic when he falls from El Capitan Mountain. It's blue when he falls and black in the close-ups. Was there a mismatch in the blue screen effect?

But the flub most noticed in all the *Star Trek* movies was a problem with the elevator shaft in "V." Watch as they pass the same floor several times on their way up. It's 35, 52, 64, 52, 77, 78, and 78 again.

KNOWING YOUR LEFT FROM YOUR RIGHT

Little gaffes and slipups often can be caused by the inattention that comes from time delays—the hours or days that can elapse between shots.

    Take, for example, Jane Fonda and Robert Redford's stroll during *Barefoot in the Park* (1967). As the pair walks away from the camera, Fonda is on Redford's right. In the very next shot, a reversal where they continue the stroll, this time facing the camera, Fonda has slipped over to his left side.

Other examples of when left isn't right and right is wrong:

Reverses—To the Second Power

Electrical devices are put on Sylvester Stallone's left temple and the left side of his chest in *Demolition Man* (1993), but when you see him frozen, the devices are on the right. In the same movie, Wesley Snipes has one blue eye and one brown eye. During a fight scene the colors are reversed.

A Director Confesses

Director Barry Sonnenfeld owned up to his own flub in *Premiere* magazine. In *Get Shorty* (1995), John Travolta parked his minivan outside Danny DeVito's house, with the van facing left. But later when Travolta, DeVito, and Rene Russo come out of the house, it's facing right. The director blamed the first shot on the director of photography who decided that the left view would look better. But in the second shot, the van had to be facing the opposite direction so DeVito could admire the remote-controlled sliding door. "I realized I had made a horrible mistake," Sonnenfeld said. But not nearly so horrible as the one owned up to by a friend of the author who discovered to his horror that in a movie he worked on, the bank robbers arrived in a red car and left in a blue one.

Wheelies

Sean Connery and Jill St. John elude pursuers by tipping a Mustang onto its right wheels and driving sideways through a narrow alley in *Diamonds Are Forever* (1971). The Mustang emerges from the alley on its two left wheels. (Since the Bond films are often replete with inside jokes, there's some speculation that the narrow alley sequence was an intentional continuity error.)

123

Say it Isn't So, Ray

Field of Dreams was one of the sleeper hits of 1989—but someone was sleeping on the mound when they let Ray Liotta, playing Shoeless Joe Jackson, bat right-handed. The real Shoeless Joe was a southpaw.

Perhaps the filmmakers should have taken a cue from veteran director Sam Wood, who had a similar problem when he worked with Gary Cooper in *Pride of the Yankees* (1942). Cooper, too, was right-handed, and he was playing Lou Gehrig, one of baseball's most famous left-handed batters. Try as he might, Cooper could not bat left-handed. Editor

Danny Mandell suggested having Cooper bat right-handed, then run to third base instead of first. Mandell merely flipped the film over in the editing room, and all was well. Of course, to make the effect work, the costumer had to sew reversed numbers on the uniforms of all the players who appeared in the shot!

Round and Round the Ferris Wheel Goes...

We have this one straight from the horse's mouth, as it were. Watch the scene at the amusement park on the pier in Steven Spielberg's *1941* (1979), and you'll see the riflemen sitting side by side on the ferris wheel swap seats as it goes around. Not only was this gaffe noticed by several erstwhile flub-spotters, but they were even alerted to it by one of the two actors who made the switch, thereby earning for himself special laurels in the Flubbie Hall of Fame.

The Surreal Thing

John Goodman, as Charlie Meadows, complains of an ear infection in *Barton Fink* (1991) and wears cotton in his right ear. But when he returns from one of his mysterious trips late in the film, he treats the infection in his left ear. Did it spread to the other side, or was it just one more of the strange aspects of the film, such as the disappearance of the bodies of the detectives after they are gunned down in the hallway? Of course, by that time surrealism has crept into the production, so just about any explanation will probably suffice.

Bridging the Gap

Dustin Hoffman should be glad he wasn't on San Francisco's Bay Bridge during the 1989 earthquake—the one that split the span between San Francisco and Berkeley. In *The Graduate* (1967), he was supposedly driving to Berkeley. But in the shots where he's on the bridge, he's heading toward San Francisco.

Physician, Reverse Thyself

Acting out the "physician, heal thyself" adage, pounced-upon medical student Kiefer Sutherland stitches up a gash on his own right cheek in *Flatliners* (1990). In the next shot, the scar is gone, then it reappears on his left cheek, where it remains for the rest of the film.

Left Side Story

As Victoria Tennant's car starts to roll away in *L.A. Story* (1991), she climbs in on the driver's side and Steve Martin on the passenger side. Yet a few minutes later when they get out at the talking highway sign, he emerges from the driver's side. Did they stop and change seats?

At Least They're in the Same Bed

Joanne Woodward's performance in *Mr. and Mrs. Bridge* (1990) is truly a wonder—a tour-de-force in seamless acting technique. But you have to wonder why while she and real-life hubby Paul Newman are in bed in the hotel in Paris, they switch sides and then switch back again. It couldn't be unbridled passion; both Mr. and Mrs. are too cool and reserved for that. At least they're in the same bed; in the old days, the Hays Office would have insisted on twin beds. And in the sequence when Paul Newman is having beer in the kitchen, isn't that a modern Budweiser label on the bottle in a scene set in the early thirties?

127

A Reversal of Bread

Claus von Bülow (Jeremy Irons), in *Reversal of Fortune* (1990), hires lawyer Alan Dershowitz (Ron Silver), and they "take a meeting" at a restaurant. Irons has a piece of bread close to his mouth, about to take a bite. In the next shot, the bread is in the same position, but he has switched hands. Silver, however, is cool to the situation. In fact, during the meal when a lemon he squeezes squirts him in the face, he holds character and doesn't react at all.

The Eye-Crossing Injury

Tom Cruise is hurt in a racetrack crash and is taken to the hospital in *Days of Thunder* (1990). His right eye is injured and you see a red ring around it. But a few scenes later, the injury has moved to his left eye.

Left Hook or Right: Either Way, an Interesting Maneuver

The traditional Captain Hook in Barrie's *Peter Pan* had a missing right hand; however, word is that Dustin Hoffman had trouble using his left hand as the operating one, so in *Hook* (1991) his left one bears the hook. This makes for an interesting situation after the invasion of Wendy's home. If a left-hooked Captain made the deep scratch up the right wall of the stairwell, then he had to either go up backward or do an intricate cross-chest maneuver to scar the right-hand wall.

At least we don't have to worry about the original Captain Hook's right hand. Word is that it found work in *The Addams Family* as "Thing."

A Flipped-Out Deer Hunter

It appears that some film was flipped in *The Deer Hunter* (1978). When Robert De Niro goes on a hunting trip, he stalks a deer in the high mountains of the Appalachians. Watch as both the bolt on his rifle and his wristwatch change sides several times. And by the way, although the scene is set in North Carolina, folks in the Northwest recognized it as Washington's Mount Baker, a 10,778-foot-high Northern Cascades behemoth. North Carolina's Mount Mitchell tops out around 6,600 feet.

Countering the Move (or Moving at the Counter)

Peter Falk and a cab driver change sides in the cutaways as they sit at a bar in *The In-Laws* (1979).

Cheeky Changeover

A dog comes over and licks Ariel's cheek as she looks over the side of the Prince's boat in *The Little Mermaid* (1989). The dog licks her right side, but she rubs her left cheek.

Cheeky Changeover II: We're Not Out of the Woods Yet

In *First Blood* (1982), a.k.a. *Rambo I*, sheriff Brian Dennehy follows Rambo (Sylvester Stallone) into the woods. Rambo surprises him pushing the sheriff up against the tree and cutting his left cheek. However, throughout the rest of the film, the cut is on his right cheek.

Did Raquel Teach the Child Left From Right?

A solicitous Tawnee Welch massages Steve Guttenberg's right leg just after he bangs it in *Cocoon* (1985). As they talk, mysteriously the left leg becomes the injured one.

Taking New Sides

At the beginning of *I Remember Mama* (1948), the "aunts" Jenny (on the right) and Sigrid (left) sit at a table drinking coffee. When Jenny asks "Where are the children?" and gets up, she and Aunt Sigrid have changed places.

GEOGRAPHY LESSONS

The nature of filmmaking is such that one city is often used to simulate another, or that a car can turn a corner in one side of town and end up miles away. To the residents of the area where the movie was filmed, it's fairly jarring, but to audiences who haven't been there, there's no reason to notice. Residents of Los Angeles, New York, and other cities which are frequent filming sites are usually enured to such happenstances, since we just assume that there was a good reason for the seamless transition from one part of town to another.

But some geographical gaffes are fairly obvious, such as the appearance of major mountains in Fort Smith, Arkansas, in *True Grit* (1969). The locals saw it and said, "No way." Likewise, many a Chicagoan noticed that when Billy Crystal and Meg Ryan leave the University of Chicago in *When Harry Met Sally* (1989), there's a bit of a local geography problem. The university is on the city's south side; yet when they leave the campus, they're next seen heading south on North Lake Shore Drive. They're heading right back to the campus. Perhaps they forgot something?

Chicagoans also had a bit of a problem with *Planes, Trains, and Automobiles* (1989), when John Candy and Steve Martin approach Chicago from the south and the landmark Sears Tower and the Presidential Towers are in the positions that they would be seen in from the north. Director John Hughes should know better. It's his hometown. And when Candy and Martin pulled over in the burned car en route to Chicago from St. Louis, they're stopped by a Wisconsin State Trooper. They must be taking the scenic route.

Near the end, when the mismatched traveling companions enter a train and it leaves the station, you can see two sets of tracks. After pondering his relationship with Candy, Martin returns on the train to the station on the same track, but exits on the same platform he just left. We're talking a fast round-trip. Or was it just a matter of running the film in reverse? Evidence exists: You can see a person walking backward on the street below the station.

So What Does a Vampire Know From Geography?

Bela Lugosi refers to the town of Whitby as "so close to London" in the 1931 *Dracula*. Whitby is 254 miles away.

Where East Meets West

The 1969 volcano epic is entitled *Krakatoa, East of Java*. Ahem. Beg pardon. The island of Krakatoa is actually *west* of Java...a problem obviously sidestepped when the videocassette release was retitled *Volcano*.

Same for You, Dick

We're happy to report that Richard Gere brought things full circle in *Final Analysis* (1992). He exits the *San Francisco* courthouse via the steps of *Los Angeles* City Hall. As an aside, your flubmeister was enroute to a meeting inside City Hall when that particular scene was being shot and had to sidestep the production crew. Little did I know at the time that I was present at the birth of a flub!

133

Eastward, Into the Setting Sun

It's a very dramatic ending...in *The Green Berets* (1968), John Wayne walks down the beach, his arm around the young Vietnamese boy, as the sun sets on the ocean behind him. Beg pardon, Mr. Wayne, sir. Perhaps you didn't realize that the beaches in Vietnam face east?

Eastward, Into the Setting Sun II (the Sequel)

The closing shot of the 1988 *Sunset* carries the supertitle: "And that's the way it really happened...Give or take a lie or two." But...in the drama of the moment, as Bruce Willis waves goodbye to James Garner, did they notice that one of the lies was that the train bearing Garner back east from Pasadena, California, was heading toward a glorious sunset over the San Gabriel Mountains, which are, of course, east of Pasadena? And so, as the sun sets in the East...

Misplacing Miss Daisy

When Hoke (Morgan Freeman) takes Miss Daisy (Jessica Tandy) into Alabama in *Driving Miss Daisy* (1989), he tells her that it's his first time outside of Georgia. But when they're met by patrolmen after they've crossed the state line, the officers are wearing Georgia State Trooper shoulder patches. An alert Georgian also noticed that not only does Hoke drive past the same house with the same truck in front of it *twice* in fifteen seconds on the way home from temple, but when he brings Miss Daisy coffee from the Krispy Kreme, it's in a styrofoam cup—something that didn't exist in the late 1950s.

The Bird Is a Traveling Turkey

A prime example of a geographical misadventure occurs in the Mel Gibson–Goldie Hawn starrer, *Bird on a Wire* (1990). Come to think of it, the very making of this movie was a misadventure. Let us talk "turkey." The couple leaves Detroit and takes a ferry to Racine, Wisconsin. As *Premiere* magazine's Terri Minsky points out, it's the kind of journey that would take a Magellan. If there were a ferry from Detroit to Racine, it would have to take the Detroit River to Lake St. Clair, continue on via the St. Clair River to Lake Huron, go all the way up Lake Huron and traverse into Lake Michigan, traveling about two-thirds of the way down to Racine. The trip would take several days at best.

MEET THE CREW

There's a perverse delight in spotting someone who really shouldn't be in a scene. From time to time, it's a casual spectator, as in *Bullitt* (1968) when, while Steve McQueen is talking to a couple of ladies in a restaurant, a man comes walking by in the background. A security guard pops into the scene and pulls him away.

More often than not, we get a brief glimpse of an actual crew member. It may be someone operating a camera which is simultaneously shooting from another direction, as in *The Fabulous Baker Boys* (1989) when the brothers Bridges fight in an alley after a bogus telethon. As the two go flying into a wire fence, you can see a man with a hand-held camera jump out of the way.

Occasionally, you'll get an inadvertent look at a crew member in a reflection in a mirror or some shiny surface. The former can be found in *Sleuth* (1972). There are supposed to be only two characters in the film, but when Laurence Olivier opens a window, you can see the reflection of a stagehand. The shiny chrome around a car mirror reveals the camera crew in Clint Eastwood's *Pink Cadillac* (1989).

More unintentional introductions:

Excuse Me, Miss...

About halfway through *Compromising Positions* (1985), when she and Judith Ivey (the "cuppycake" lady) are riding in a car, Susan Sarandon gets a dialogue cue when a finger comes from the back seat and taps her on the shoulder.

Sticking It to the Bear

A bear crashes through a door, which falls atop John Candy in *The Great Outdoors* (1988). As the bear bounces on the door, the trainer's yellow stick can be seen poking at it.

A Helping Hand for the Batmobile

When Michael Keaton calls for the Batmobile in *Batman* (1989), the car supposedly starts up by itself and drives up an alley. As John McLaughlin would say on TV, "Wrong!" In one of the front shots, a hand can be seen on the steering wheel.

The Not-So-Hidden Camera

When the characters in *Sweet Heart's Dance* (1988) go on a tropical vacation, there's a scene on a hotel balcony where you can see another camera crew, shooting the reverses, facing directly toward the camera that's filming the action.

A Hairy Moment

Elizabeth Taylor is supposedly alone in the room when she stands in front of a mirror in *Butterfield 8* (1960). But you can briefly see a crew member's hairy arm in the mirror.

More Than One Debut

Bad Boys (1983) starred Sean Penn and was Ally Sheedy's screen debut. But was it also the cameraman's screen debut? Look for him in the fight sequence at the end of the movie, standing with a hand-held camera in the group of kids that circle the action.

Along for the Ride

In the final scene of *The Road Warrior* (1981), Mel Gibson is driving a tanker, and everyone is wearing post-holocaust attire—except in an interior shot, where a cameraman in 1980s garb films the getaway.

141

Wandering Past Its Own Reflection

As the camera wanders around Sean Connery's apartment building in *The Untouchables* (1987), it not only catches the action—it catches itself. Both the crane and crew can be seen in a reflection in a window.

Was the Crew Dancing, Too?

In *Xanadu* (1980), during Olivia Newton-John and Gene Kelly's song and dance number, "Whenever You're Away From Me," there's a moment when the vocals have stopped and they're dancing to the music. As they go past a large mirror you can see the film crew.

Rats! They Saw Me!

As Bruce Davison is mixing Ben the rat's food with poison in the kitchen in *Willard* (1981), you can see a trainer who is putting Willard on his mark reflected in one of the glass doors.

The Not-So-Secret Hiding Place

As Pee-wee Herman (a.k.a. Paul Reubens) waters the lawn near the beginning of *Pee-wee's Big Adventure* (1985), he enters a secret code to access his bike's hiding place. A door opens, and if you'll look closely at the left side of the garage, a leg moves quickly out of the shot.

Everything That Goes Around ...

Shortly after a big musical number in *Beaches* (1988), Bette Midler and Barbara Hershey go into an apartment building through revolving doors. As the door spins around, look for the camera crew in a shiny reflection.

Walk on By

Director Harry Beaumont must have let things get a little sloppy on the set of *The Floradora Girl* (1930), starring Marion Davies. At one point, a crew member walks right in front of the camera; on another, you can see the clapboard. Or was Davies's sugar daddy William Randolph Hearst hanging around the set and making Beaumont nervous?

He Didn't Get Out Fast Enough

During a struggle in Charlie Sheen's room in *The Rookie* (1989) between his wife and the bad guys, as they spin around the room the camera catches a brief glimpse of one of the crew.

The musical *Seven Brides for Seven Brothers* (1954) features several lavish Michael Kidd numbers, including one where the brothers are dancing outside their rustic house. On the right in the background, you can see the knees and feet of several stagehands working above the set.

143

Sneaking a Peak

We couldn't expect you to be overly attentive to detail during a scene in Brian DePalma's *Body Double* (1984) when a porn movie is being filmed. But check out the mirror on the door in Melanie Griffith's room for a brief glimpse of the camera crew. On the other hand, give DePalma and cinematographer Stephen H. Burum credit for being able to pull off a scene that was fraught with opportunities for error in a scene when the camera takes a 360° spin. In that instance, a special rig was built to carry the camera crew and the actors for the merry-go-round effect.

We're Just Looking for a Book

Michael Douglas is in the library in *Fatal Attraction* (1987) talking with Stuart Pankin about the affair with Glenn Close when an employee pushes a cart of books past a French door—with the camera crew mirrored in it.

Dances With Wolves

Dances With Wolves (1990) is a fine, fine movie. That's why it troubles us so much to have to point out a few of its flubs. But we have our work to do, and we continue undaunted.

Perhaps the most notable of its glitches happens when the wagon driver Timmons (Robert Pastorelli) takes John Dunbar (Kevin Costner) to the cavalry outpost. It's one of those instances where the old saying about getting egg on one's face becomes cinematic reality. The driver takes a bite of a pickled egg, then when Costner tells him to leave him at the abandoned fort, he spews it out, getting some on his mustache. Then he looks over to Costner, and the egg is gone. In the next shot, it's back again.

And speaking of Timmons, one person who saw the movie wondered why the Indians could down a bison with a single arrow, but it took four to kill Timmons. And even after he's dead and scalped, he appears to take a breath.

We wondered about Mary McDonnell's hair. In the first

place, it changes length in the scene when Dunbar first finds her mourning the death of her husband. But even more important, if, as the story says, she has lived with the Indians since she was a child, how come she's the only one with a shag hairdo? Why isn't her hair styled like the rest of the Indian women?

Another alert flub spotter noticed that when the soldiers are cleaning their rifles, one is wearing a wedding ring—a tradition that didn't come along until much later. There was also much discussion of Costner's use of the rather modern expression, "Hi!"

We leave with a couple of notes from experts in their field, who also found minute details which caught their eye. One hunter noticed a feather from a ring-necked pheasant in an Indian's headdress, saying that the bird wouldn't have been in that part of the country during the era of the movie. Another noticed that when the flock of birds flies overhead, the sound effect is that of Canadian Honkers, but the birds are actually Sandhill Cranes. And an apple grower reported that a partly-eaten Red Delicious apple is seen in the Civil War scene. The Red Delicious is a treat that didn't appear until around 1900. And, hey, how come the dead wolf seems to be wearing a choke chain collar? Our flub spotters know their stuff.

MIRACULOUS HEALINGS AND WONDROUS CLEAN-UPS

Part of the natural process of making a motion picture is to film scenes out of sequence. The movie that you see on the screen is a montage of scenes that were filmed for economies of scale, scheduling, and availability of actors. Quite often much more of the story was filmed than what you see on the screen in order to fit into a specific running time. Thus all of the scenes that are planned for a specific set may well be filmed together on that set, even though they appear at different points in the film.

A car that is damaged in scene "A" might well appear on screen undamaged in scene "B." The magic of the cinematic repair job is especially evident in *Smokey and the Bandit* (1977), when the sheriff Jackie Gleason's car goes through several wrecks and mysterious restorations.

In a similar case, in *Commando* (1985), Arnold Schwarzenegger, driving Rae Dawn Chong's car, rams a yellow Porsche several times during a chase, causing it to be badly dented. Later, when he drops the bad guy

off a cliff and gets into the car and drives off, the dents have miraculously disappeared—only to reappear later. When the film ràn on television, thousands of viewers marveled at the repair job. Earl Scheib should do so well.

While we're at it, we should also point out that Arnold has more than one vehicular problem in *Commando*. When he pushes a disabled pickup truck down a hill to chase his daughter's kidnappers, white smoke emits from its exhaust pipe. Not bad for an engine that wouldn't start. And when he's in the mall parking garage and hits the Porsche, his wallet falls to the ground. He jumps into a red convertible and drives off without picking up the wallet. A short while later, he shows Rae Dawn Chong a picture of his daughter that is in the wallet he left on the floor of the garage.

At any rate, the nonsequential shooting schedule not only can heal dents in cars, it can clean clothes, change hairstyles, and rebuild buildings.

It's time for some testimony:

Over the River and Through the Woods, To Grandma's Washer We Go

There must be a laundromat hidden somewhere in the woods in *Deliverance* (1972). Jon Voight decides to kill something for breakfast. While away from camp, he spots a deer, then trips and tumbles down a small hill. He's covered with leaves and dirt, but when he gets back to camp, he's clean as a whistle.

The Door to Cleanliness

Things get pretty vicious when Jim Morrison (Val Kilmer) and his girlfriend Pamela (Meg Ryan) argue at a Thanksgiving dinner in *The Doors* (1991). She throws food at him (apparently mashed yams) which splatters on his face and his clothes. As the argument continues, the mess remains on his clothes, but his face is scrubbed spotless.

A Merciful Clean-up

Kim Basinger undergoes a quick clean-up in a scene with Richard Gere in *No Mercy* (1986). In one shot she has dirt on her face, in the next she's almost clean, then dirty, then clean.

The Stainless Wife

After a battle in *Total Recall* (1990), Arnold Schwarzenegger is covered with blood. He confronts his wife (Sharon Stone), grabbing her shoulders with his bloody hands. But they leave no stains on her shoulders.

153

More Notes on the Healing of Windshields

An automobile windshield is the subject of a quick healing in *Narrow Margin* (1990). Gene Hackman and Anne Archer are being chased by a sniper in a helicopter who shoots and breaks the windshield of their truck. But in the next shot, from the interior of the car, the windshield is just fine. Same thing happens in *The Godfather* (1972). When Sonny Corleone (James Caan) is ambushed by hit men, the very first shots completely shatter the windshield. He escapes, only to be riddled with bullets. After one of the hit men kicks him, there's a cut to shots which show the devastation on the toll station. Then there's a shot of the car on which we can see the bullet holes, but the windshield is still intact. And in *Cujo* (1983), when the dog attacks a mother and child, a broken windshield is suddenly restored.

The Cleaned-Up Racer

Dave Stoller falls from his bike in the last race of *Breaking Away* (1979), and his T-shirt gets pretty dirty. But when he crosses the finish line, he has obviously stopped and changed into a fresh, clean T-shirt.

The Crane Stains

Bob Crane fights with an artist and gets paint on his suit and face in Disney's *Superdad* (1974), but the stains on both change shape and size from shot to shot.

The Wizard of Oz

We're off to see the Wizard. As we go down the Yellow Brick Road, it's time to look for some film flubs and other glitches in a movie that's probably been seen by more people on the planet Earth than anything Hollywood has ever produced. As such, it opens the door to many a flub-spotting expedition, with so many folks looking at it so closely. But the interesting thing is that you're so charmed by the story that the flubs can just slip on by. But we'd better get started, before the Wicked Witch finds us.

In the early sepia-toned scenes, Auntie Em is taking some chickens out of the incubator. She counts "sixty-seven, sixty-eight, sixty-nine." She then puts three more in her apron and takes one from Dorothy, counting, "seventy." It should have been seventy-three.

Dorothy has one heck of a dry cleaner. First, when she falls into the pigpen, she doesn't get dirty. Later, she has two spots on her dress when she's on the dirt road talking to Toto, but in the next scene, she's clean.

155

An oil lamp that was on the table by the window earlier has disappeared before the window is blown open by the storm; and when her bed is sliding all over the room during the tornado and pictures are moving about on the walls, notice that bottles on the table don't even move.

There's an interesting situation with the background footage during the tornado scene. The background that you see when Auntie Em and the farmhands go into the storm cellar is different from that when Dorothy tries to enter it a few moments later. It appears to be the footage we saw when Dorothy comes into the house through the front door.

There's another interesting switcheroo when Dorothy is watching the action outside the window as the house flies through the air. It's clear that there is a curtained window behind her, yet when the house lands, the window's gone, replaced by a wall with a bundt cake pan hanging on.

Throughout the film, Dorothy can't seem to hang on to sweets. Early on, the cruller she's eating disappears before she sings "Over the Rainbow." Then we never discover what happens to the lollipop (brought on by our buddy Jerry Maren) and flowers that she had in her hand after Glenda the Good Witch leaves.

All sorts of things go awry when Dorothy and friends are in the Witch's Castle. In the first place, notice that the sign pointing the way is misspelled. It says "Witches Castle." Next, the Tin Man chops down the door with an ax he didn't have as he climbed the stairs. And, as Dorothy and pals run down the stairs, they start out as Scarecrow, Dorothy, Tin Woodsman, and the Lion. There is a quick cut to the cackling witch, then the order is Scarecrow, Tin Woodsman, Dorothy, and the Lion.

Another point to ponder is that it's always the brainless Scarecrow who seems to come up with the ideas that get them out of a jam.

Before the Wicked Witch of the West sends her flying monkeys to capture Dorothy and friends in the Haunted Forest, a line of dialogue was mistakenly left in. She tells the head monkey that she has "sent a little insect on ahead to

take the fight out of them." This refers to a song-and-dance sequence featuring "The Jitterbug," a little insect that causes its victims to dance wildly until they are exhausted. The sequence was cut from the film after preview showings—but you can see it on the laserdisc version of the movie.

Just before meeting the Cowardly Lion, Dorothy, the Tin Man, and the Scarecrow head down the road, singing "We're Off to See the Wizard." Something is going on in the background that has engendered one of those strange film legends. Indeed you can see a figure moving about among the scenery trees just beyond the little house that sits beside the road. It appears to be a crew member who was caught on the set when the camera was running. The word that was circulating among those who choose to believe it was that a crew member had actually committed suicide on the set, hanging himself from the tree.

C'mon, now. Do you think if that was indeed the case, Hollywood could have kept it quiet all these years? This is a town where everything is public knowledge. Everything. It's a town where an out-of-work actress named Peg Entwhistle became the stuff of legend when she committed suicide by jumping off the "H" of the HOLLYWOOD sign. Where Jon Erik Hexum made worldwide headlines when he accidentally killed himself on the set of his TV show. Where every sordid moment of filmdom's past has been exposed by books such as Kenneth Anger's *Hollywood Babylon,* by the Grave Line Tours, and God knows whatall else.

We even went so far as to check with a leading authority on the movie, Aljean Harmetz, the respected *New York Times* reporter who wrote the book, *The Making of "The Wizard of Oz."* She said that if it had ever happened, it was news to her.

Granted, there were some serious production problems on the set. The Wicked Witch (Margaret Hamilton) was so badly burned in a special effects accident that she had to be hospitalized, and Buddy Ebsen, originally cast to play the Tin Woodsman, nearly died from the effects of the silver makeup.

Other little *Oz* flubs we noticed:

The Cowardly Lion's "crown," made from a broken flower pot, bounces when it falls from his head at the end of "If I Were King of the Forest."

When the Scarecrow gets his diploma, he shows off his newfound brainpower with the statement: "The sum of the square roots of any two sides of an isosceles triangle is equal to the square root of the remaining side." Ahem. Wrong. So much for the Scarecrow's intellect. David Fradkin points out in *Los Angeles* magazine that in the Pythagorean theorem, the square of the length of the hypotenuse (longest side) of a *right* triangle is equal to the sum of the *squares* of the lengths of the other two sides.

NOBODY NOTICED

Filmdom's trickiest continuity gaffes are the little things that no one seemed to notice at the time—ones spotted by only the most eagle-eyed moviegoer. Usually, they're the things of today that just don't make sense in the films of yesteryear.

As an example, look closely at the cavewomen in the 1966 *One Million Years B.C.* with Raquel Welch. Isn't it interesting that even back then they were able to buy false eyelashes? Apparently, you have to look your best to get a caveman to bash you over your head and drag you by the hair into his lair.

Bachelor Party

Billy Wilder's *Double Indemnity* (1944) is one of filmdom's great classics—but it also contains a classic example of the little things that seem to slip by. Even though Fred MacMurray has been established as a carefree, never-married bachelor, throughout the entire film he wears a wide gold wedding band.

In This Vale of Tears

Vicki Vale's name is spelled "Vicky Vale" on the cover of a magazine featuring her photographs in the 1989 *Batman*. And in another Jack Nicholson flick, during the course of *The Shining* (1980), the first name of the previous caretaker changes.

Holy Bat Gaffe

When Jack Nicholson as the Joker and his evil band are vandalizing paintings in *Batman* (1989), one villian puts pink handprints all over a portrait. In the next shot, the handprints have disappeared.

Gonna Make My Brown Eyes Blue

In a flashback in the 1989 *Batman*, the young Jack Nicholson has blue eyes. The later Jack Nicholson has brown eyes!

Miraculous Disappearance

And in the same *Batman*, police lieutenant Eckhardt appears at the gate outside the Axis Chemical Company with a stubble of beard. Moments later, he's inside the plant—clean shaven.

Transcendent and Translucent

The special effects which blend flying birds with human actors in Alfred Hitchcock's *The Birds* (1963) are remarkable...so remarkable, in fact, that when assembling the special effects for a sequence set on a sunny day in one scene, no one noticed that the creatures that chase the children cast no shadows!

Feats of Extreme Gravity

Well, let's face it. Stanley Kubrick couldn't shoot *2001—A Space Odyssey* (1968) in a weightless environment, so he just had to make do with special effects to get all the floating objects and people to look right in his meticulously-crafted masterpiece. However, even this classic is not without its oversights. Look for the time when Floyd sucks some liquid food from a container—and the remainder of the liquid drops back to the bottom, just as it would in earth's gravity. There's also a scene at the Orbiter Hilton where it appears that William Sylvester is blowing the food down the straw rather than sucking it up.

And at another point in the movie, the captain leans on the back of Floyd's chair. No mean feat in an environment where gravity isn't pulling on your own feet. Also—when an astronaut leaves the pod in a free-float to work on the AE35 unit, you can see the shadow of the cables attached to his feet.

Putting Out the Lights

In 1995's *Toy Story*, Woody hides in a pile of Christmas lights. He darts out of hiding to grab Buzz Lightyear, and when they return to the hallway, the lights have disappeared. But when he decides to use the string of lights to climb out the window, they're right back just when he needs them.

165

The Future Is in the Background

In the 1983 Spanish production of *Carmen*, the time frame of course, is the 1800s. As the gypsies dance around the campfire, the lights of Seville brighten in the background as a helicopter arrives with its landing lights blazing.

A Burning Question

Did anyone notice that as Ginger Rogers teases Fred Astaire with "A Fine Romance" in *Swing Time* (1936), he takes a few puffs on his pipe then puts it—lit—in his jacket pocket? David Hajdu did, and wonders how Fred stayed so cool during the rest of the number.

License to Kill

John Carpenter's horror classic *Halloween* (1978) is set in a town in Illinois. How many noticed that the cars have California license plates?

The Six...er, Seven Shooter

Donald Pleasence as "Loomis" fires six shots at the Michael Myers creature in the 1978 *Halloween*. But when the moment is recalled in a flashback in the sequel, *Halloween II* (1981), Pleasence fires seven shots in the exact same scene.

Footprints in the Snows of Time

When Ronald Colman gets lost in a blizzard in the mountains of Tibet in Frank Capra's 1937 classic *Lost Horizon*, he rolls down a mountain on which "no man" has ever set foot. But, if that's true, what's the explanation for a long set of footprints in the snow in the foreground of the shot?

No Flossing on Krypton

The subject: Christopher Reeve's portrayal of *Superman* (1978). Our hero may well be invincible—able to leap tall buildings in a single bound and to fend off bullets with his "S"-embossed chest—but obviously, he was no match for the dentist. The Man of Steel has fillings in his teeth.

At the Drop of a Hat

A super-sensitive floor is a key plot device in *Treasure of the Four Crowns* (1983). But when a hat is dropped on it, no one noticed that the alarm didn't go off!

Circle the Winnebagos

John Wayne was a busy man being both star and director of *The Alamo* (1960). So can we blame him if he didn't notice that mobile trailers appear in the background of several battle scenes...or that we can see a falling stunt man land on a mattress?

Stock Pot-Shots

Many a moviemaker uses "stock footage"—existing film—to build a scene. Rather than go out and shoot a particular scene—especially something such as an "establishing shot" that shows a view of a city, street scenes, cloud shots, and so forth—a producer or director (or one of their flunkies) can buy the footage from a stock supplier or go back into the studio vaults. That's what special effects genius George Pal did once upon a time. However, when *War of the Worlds* (1953) and *When Worlds Collide* (1951) were shown on a double bill in the late 1950s, the audience was treated to seeing the same group of people sitting in the same store listening to the same radio telling of the approach of impending doom in both movies.

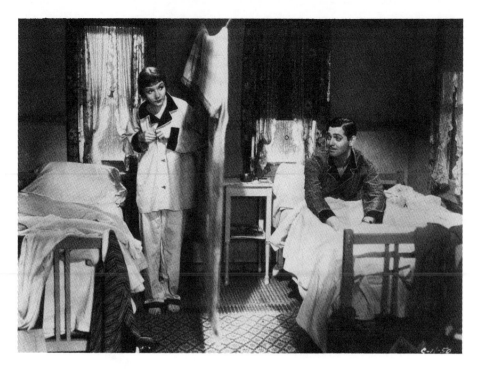

Time Stands Still

In *It Happened One Night* (1934), Clark Gable leaves Claudette Colbert in a tourist cabin. The clock on the wall indicates that it's 2:30 in the morning. He drives to New York, writes a story for the newspaper, and drives back. When he later returns to the room, the clock still reads 2:30. (Of course, he could have been gone *exactly* 24 hours!)

170

Shooting Gallery

Classic scenes in classic films aren't immune to little background flubs. In Hitchcock's *North by Northwest* (1959), there's a wonderful bit early on in the restaurant scene. A small boy is seated with his family at a table in the background. *Before* Eva Marie Saint reaches into her purse to pull out a gun and shoot Cary Grant, the prescient little boy grimaces and puts his finger in his ears to avoid the noise. (Undoubtedly he remembered from rehearsals that there's a big bang coming.)

Come Fly With Me

In the 1956 film *Carousel*, set in 1870, a World War II airplane flies across the Booth Bay Harbor. Probably flying Frank Sinatra out—or replacement Gordon MacRae in.

High Noon in Hollywood

There's a crane shot in *High Noon* (1952) that starts with Gary Cooper and pans up to show the empty streets. But the camera pulls back a bit too far, and you see beyond that set to telephone poles in the background. And, by the way, did anyone notice the changing of the town newspaper? Sometimes it's the *Chronicle*, at others it's the *Clarion*.

Perhaps He Should Stick Out His Thumb

While a pursued Cornel Wilde searches for food in darkest Africa in *The Naked Prey* (1966), a car drives by in the background. (Just a thought: With the change of just one letter, this title could become a movie about Sunday morning in a nudist colony.)

Traffic Management

An assistant director can be seen in a jeep waving the extras on in the 1956 *War and Peace*. Wrong war!

Day for Night

Movie sound man John Travolta wrecks his car while rushing to save Nancy Allen in Brian De Palma's *Blow Out* (1981). It's broad daylight when he is pulled from the wreckage and put in an ambulance. But just seconds later, he hears Allen screaming through his earphone. He jumps out of the ambulance to save her—and day has turned to night.

A Dangerous Business

Show business is a painful business for one of the dancers in *There's No Business Like Show Business* (1954). During the "Heat Wave" number, Marilyn Monroe accidentally hits one of the male dancers across the face with her hand.

She's Ba-a-ack!

They just can't get rid of Cher in one scene of *Silkwood* (1983). In the latter part of the film, when the house is plundered by the men searching for radiation, Karen (Meryl Streep) and Dolly (Cher) are questioned, then Dolly is escorted into a waiting car an taken away. But not long afterward, in a close shot of Karen, you can see Dolly slightly out of focus, still in the background.

Glasnost Take the Hind Most

In *Rambo III* (1988), Sly Stallone steals a Russian "Hind" helicopter just after he releases his Green Beret commander (Richard Crenna) and some Afghan rebels from their cells. Watch as the "Russian" helicopter revs up and you'll see a small American flag on its rotor housing.

Any Old Port in a Storm

The Maltese Falcon (1941) is set in San Francisco…but, like most movies, was filmed largely in Los Angeles. Thus, when the La Paloma burns, a sign reading "Port of Los Angeles" is seen over a door leading onto a wharf.

175

Getting Glare in Your Eyes

Early in the classic Western *Shane* (1953), Alan Ladd is riding across a field. In the distance is a fast-moving glare, obviously the sun reflecting from the windshield of a speeding car. In the same film, look for Elisha Cook, Jr.'s body to move around from shot to shot as he lies dead in the mud.

Sneak Preview

"Product Placement" has become a near and dear technique in modern moviemaking. This is the prominent display of products in a film, providing the manufacturer has ponied up a hunk of change for the privilege. Nowhere is it more prominent than in Universal's *Back to the Future* trilogy, films which are at times one long commercial. But Warner Bros. is not without the stain of sin. In the 1990 *My Blue Heaven*, a theater marquee in the background advertises Warner's *White Hunter, Black Heart*, the Clint Eastwood film to be released later in the year.

Three Men and a Baby (The Ghost Story)

It's one of the best things that ever happened to video rentals. Somebody started one of those strange rumors about the appearance of a ghost in *Three Men and a Baby* (1987) and word spread. All over America people were rushing to rent or buy the video so they could see the ghost. Let's have a little talk about it.

Here's what you'll see: When Celeste Holm goes toward the baby's crib, she passes a floor-to-ceiling window in which you see nothing. She picks up the baby and walks back past the window as she talks to Ted Danson. This time there's what appears to be a little boy peeking in on the scene.

A rumor got started that this was the ghost of a little boy who had died in the house where the movie was said to be filmed. It became one of those stories that everyone wanted to believe. The Disney switchboard was inundated. I talked to the person who had to take most of the calls, and she said she was nearly driven nuts. People didn't believe the official explanation. They wanted to believe what they wanted to believe.

She's the same person, incidentally, who had to take the calls when someone thought they saw an erect penis drawn into the towers of the castle on the poster and cassette cover of *The Little Mermaid*. She said that there were days when she felt like answering the phone "Penis Central." And, in case you're wondering, it sorta looks like that's what it is, but I'm sure it's accidental. (No commercial artist who ever wants to work again would try to pull off a trick like that.)

Anyway, back to the topic. Touchstone (the Disney division that produced the picture) maintains, as the official company explanation, that what you see in *Three Men and a Baby* is a portion of a cardboard cutout of Ted Danson wearing a fez, a prop that would tie in with his role as a flamboyant commercial actor/model. Touchstone says it was put into place accidentally. That's the party line.

The entire situation is ripe with fallacies. In the first place, even if you do believe in ghosts, you have to accept that tenet that they can't be photographed. There's nothing there of the kind of substance that would reflect light into a camera.

Second, even though the "ghost" story makes a good one, the scene was *not* shot in an apartment in New York where a small child had died. It was shot on a soundstage in Toronto. It was a movie set, and no one had ever died on that stage.

Third, it's too hard to keep secrets on a set. There are just too many people involved. If that had been a ghost, if it had been verifiable as a ghost, if there was any substance to the story (or the image) at all, it doubtless would have been front-page news in every paper in the country. Trust me. And if you don't trust me, remember that Leonard Nimoy directed the movie. He would have told us. Vulcans can't lie.

I'll have to say that Der Flubmeister here doesn't buy the entire Touchstone line on the incident. I've looked at the tape several times, and I feel that it really is a little boy. A real, live, flesh and blood child who happened to be on the set and peeked in through the window, getting caught by the camera. The "cutout" story seems fairly fallacious to me.

At any rate, whatever it is, it is indeed a film flub. It's something that shouldn't have been on the film, shouldn't have been seen, shouldn't have broken the story line. And I'll believe it's a ghost the same day that I have proof that a UFO lands at Harvard and the denizens chat with an astronomy prof, instead of landing in a swamp and kidnapping a hillbilly.

NOW YOU SEE IT, NOW YOU DON'T

One of the results of stitching a film together from various non-sequential takes is that things can disappear before your eyes. Now you see it, now you don't. They're among the more amusing flubs to locate—ones that certainly make you suspend your suspension of disbelief and snap right back to reality.

More often than not, it takes a bravura flub-spotter to catch the little disappearances. They're rarely so obvious as to slap you in the face ... well, maybe they are. Let's venture into the thin air:

He Took It Back

One of the plot points in *Gardens of Stone* (1987) is the importance to Jackie Willow (D. B. Sweeney) of the Combat Infantryman's Badge. At Willow's funeral, Hazard (James Caan) mentions this fact, then makes a great show of ripping off his own badge and placing it on the casket. But, in the next scene the badge is still pinned to Hazard's chest for the eulogy.

Earl Scheib Is There When You Need Him

Farrah Fawcett drives a badly-dented Datsun as she is chased through the streets of Acapulco in the 1979 *Sunburn*. The chase leads right into a *corrida*. The Datsun disappears into a tunnel, and emerges into the bull-ring with nary a scratch or dent. Also, in the lobby card for this comedy, it's easy to see the cameraman sitting in the front seat next to Farrah.

Fooled Us

In *Nobody's Fool* (1994), Paul Newman drives away with a stolen lawnmower in the back of his pickup truck. A few shots later there's no lawnmower. The truck bed is empty, but then the lawnmower returns.

Fingering the Killer

The jewelry gremlins did a bit of sabotage to Alfred Hitchcock's 1936 spy thriller *Sabotage*. During a scene in which Sylvia Sidney plots to kill Oscar Homolka with a carving knife, you can see a ring on the third finger of her left hand. A few frames later, the ring is gone.

Missing Children

When Thomas Mitchell makes his speech in church in *High Noon* (1952), there are children sitting in the pews along with the adults. Then the children mysteriously disappear, but they're back in the next shot. Thank the Lord.

A Tall Order

Super-sized Kevin Peter Hall as the clumsy Bigfoot monster crashes his head through the Hendersons' ceiling in the 1987 *Harry and the Hendersons*. But in the next scene, the ceiling is in perfect condition.

Fried Skivvies

When Demi Moore tosses Woody Harrelson's dirty laundry around the kitchen in *Indecent Proposal* (1993), a pair of shorts lands on the stove, right by a steaming tea kettle. A wide shot then shows that the skivvies have vanished, but they're miraculously back in place in time to catch afire a short while later.

183

A Messy Flub

A drooling Bruce Willis is on the floor of his cell in the opening of *Twelve Monkeys* (1995), but in one shot the drool disappears, only to return in the next shot.

Tiny Footprints on the Shirt

Either they had come up with the formula for disappearing paint, or there was a laundromat in Never-Never Land. In *Hook* (1991), when a grown-up Peter Pan (Robin Williams) arrives there, the Lost Boys shoot him with plungers filled with a fluid that stains his shirt. Then Tinker Bell (Julia Roberts) walks all over him, literally. When he returns home, he still has the tiny footprints on his shirt, but the stains are gone.

And while we're speaking of things that vanish, did you notice that the family flies to England on Pan Am Airways, which had itself disappeared by the time the movie was released?

Make Mine Dry, Please

Chevy Chase jumps fully clothed into a lake in *Funny Farm* (1988), then wades out and gets into his car. In the next scene, his clothes are miraculously dry. Dry too are Michael Caine's, when, after swimming to damsel-in-distress Lorraine Gary's rescue in *Jaws the Revenge* (1987), he climbs into her boat without a drop of water on him and with his shirt still neatly pressed.

Food and the Beast

Food must be in the eyes of the beholder. There's a scene in *Beauty and the Beast* (1991) when the Beast gets food on his face while having trouble with table manners. But when Belle ("Beauty") looks at him, he's clean. Then the food's back again. Food also comes and goes from Ogre's face during a pie-eating scene in *Revenge of the Nerds* (1984). Gosh, you try and try to teach Beasts and Ogres good manners and what thanks do you get?

Beauty and the Books

Something also happens to the first book that Belle puts in her basket in the aforementioned *Beauty and the Beast* (1991). It disappears. Yet when a lamb bites a piece from another book, the bite pops right back in—shades of Julia Robert's gambit with the pancake in *Pretty Woman* (1990).

185

Licking the Lost Child

One of the saddest disappearances happens in *Bambi* (1942). When the animals are on the other side of the river after having fled the forest fire, a mother raccoon licks her baby—then it vanishes, leaving her licking the air. But in another instance, there's a mother-and-child reunion when Bambi's mom is leading him through the wilderness. She momentarily disappears, then reappears again. Still another loss occurs when a flock of crows is flying across the screen and about eight of them simply vanish.

Did They Steal Tom Cruise's Famous Jockey Shorts, Too?

During one of the final scenes of *Risky Business* (1983), a moving van can be seen filled with furniture. But it appears that someone made a quick heist. As the van drives away, it is empty.

The Changing Family Dynamic

A real case of "now you see it, now you don't" happens in Jane Fonda and Robert De Niro's *Stanley and Iris* (1990). Two characters—Iris's sister Sharon (Swoosie Kurtz) and Sharon's husband Joe (Jamey Sheridan)—disappear halfway through the picture, without explanation. Turns out that it was due to the director's changing his mind about the family dynamic. Director Martin Ritt told Rob Medich in *Premiere* magazine that he cut them out because of a scene where Sharon finds her husband having sex with Iris's daughter Kelly (Martha Plimpton). He wanted to change the way things worked within the family. Now that's an understatement!

Sleigh Bells Ring/Don't Ring, Are You Listening?

When the reindeer is released at the end of *Prancer* (1990), first it's wearing sleigh bells, then it isn't, then it is again.

A Quick Cleanup in a Galaxy Far, Far Away

The cup of tea which Captain Sulu (George Takai) drinks in *Star Trek VI* (1991) crashes to the floor when the spaceship is attacked. Sulu falls also, but by the time he gets up, the cleanup crew must have made a fast trip onto the set, because the pieces of the shattered cup and saucer have vanished.

Noah Gets Lost

A character disappears during the course of the classic *The Grapes of Wrath* (1940). Tom Joad (Henry Fonda) has a semi-retarded younger brother Noah (Frank Sully) who is part of the story up until the swimming-in-the-river scene after which we never see him again. In the book Noah feels he's a burden and runs away; in the movie, there's no explanation for his disappearance.

Cleaning Up the Act of Love

Preludes to cinematic lovemaking can be a pretty messy business, yet, if properly messy, can become far more sensual than seeing the act itself. Take, for example, the famous chicken-eating scene between Joyce Redman and Albert Finney in *Tom Jones* (1963). There's never been a porn film that could convey that kind of sensuality as the pair lasciviously devour a roast chicken. You know exactly what's going to happen next, even though there's never a hint of anything vaguely pornographic. Similarly, the sequence in *Ghost* (1990) wherein Demi Moore and Patrick Swayze turn the making of a clay pot into a phallic extravaganza of love and desire. Of course, they get frightfully messy— but when they turn away from the potter's wheel to paw each other as a prelude to hopping into bed, they do so with clean hands and clothes as the clay magically disappears.

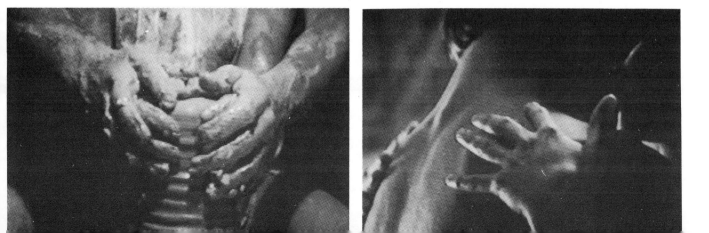

Somebody Licked It Off

The icing magically disappears off a cake in *Three Men and a Little Lady* (1990). Nancy Travis turns baker, tries to piece the broken cake together, and then puts chocolate icing on it. But in the next scene when she brings it to the counter all the icing is gone.

Fast Evaporation in the Summer Heat

Daryl Hannah goes up to the bar at a garden party in *Steel Magnolias* (1989), where she meets her future husband. He hands her a drink, full to the brim. When she takes it from him, however, it has lost about an inch of its contents.

Numbers Lost and Found

In *What's Eating Gilbert Grape* (1993), as Mary Steenburgin talks to Johnny Depp in the grocery store just after her husband's funeral, the cash register reads $63.69. In the next shot it shows a balance of $0.00, and in the next it's $63.69 again.

Numbers Found and Lost

In *White Men Can't Jump* (1992), Rosie Perez builds up her *Jeopardy* score to $5100, answers a question correctly taking it up to $8300, then in the next shot it has mysteriously dropped to $5100 again.

Food Fights

Look for a mound of whipped cream to vanish from Charles Durning's pumpkin pie in *Home for the Holidays* (1995) quicker than the portly actor could possibly slurp it down. Later, when the juicy stuffed turkey is dumped on Holly Hunter's cinematic sister, Cynthia Stevenson, the actress's hair is a mess in one shot, nice and clean in the next, then turkeyed up again in the next.

Clean Dancing

The ever-fastidious Patrick Swayze, in the final dance scene of *Dirty Dancing* (1987), jumps from the stage and makes a dramatic slide across the floor on his knees. When he stands up, the knees of his black trousers are smudged, but in the next shot, they're clean and crisply pressed.

Scared the Hat Right Off His Head

Winston (Ernie Hudson) gets his hat scared right off him in *Ghostbusters II* (1989). He, Egon (Harold Ramis) and Ray (Dan Aykroyd) are in the subway tunnel, all wearing hard hats until they are frightened by some corpseless heads and Winston's hat comes and goes as they are screaming.

NUMBERS GAME

Most of the time, when there's a juicy little film flub, it's not too difficult to ferret out the cause—whether a mistake on the part of someone in the crew, an oversight, something that wasn't researched carefully enough, or a moment of inattention. Then again, some flubs really don't have any logical explanation.

Six Plus Six Equals Seventeen

When Sundance (Robert Redford) reloads his two six-shooters in a gun battle in *Butch Cassidy and the Sundance Kid* (1969), he then gets off at least seventeen shots.

They'll Never Find Him Now

In an episode of TV's *Quantum Leap,* Sam Beckett (Scott Bakula) is living in the Watts area of Los Angeles during the 1960s riots. He asks Al (Dean Stockwell) where his (Sam's) apartment is. Al tells him that it's 218, but in the next scene, when Sam is in the apartment and the outside door is opened, it's 217.

A Baker's Dozen of Miscounts

There are only ten women in *Thirteen Women* (1932), a movie about a girl (Myrna Loy) of mixed racial heritage out to avenge childhood mistreatment by murdering her tormentors. But, just to make up for the slight, *Her Twelve Men* (1954) has Greer Garson teaching a private-school class of thirteen boys.

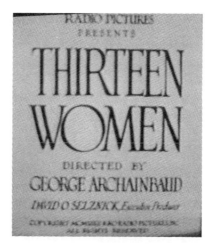

One More Time

A bad guy with a six-shooter takes aim at Tommy Lee Jones in *Black Moon Rising* (1986) ... and fires seven shots.

Missing Oranges

About halfway through *Out of Africa* (1985), while on a camping trip, Meryl Streep and Robert Redford are sitting around a campfire during a night scene and he's peeling an orange. Even though it appears that he's peeling only one, the number of oranges in the bowl on the camp table keeps changing.

The Question Is: Where is the Address?

When Rob Morrow is tracking down Herb Stempel in *Quiz Show* (1995), he lists the address as 1066-55 17th Avenue in Queens. A later closeup shows the address as 106-55 19th Street. But when Morrow visits Stempel, the address is 2177.

Time Travel

The baby carriage scene in *The Untouchables* (1987) begins a little after 5:00, so says the clock on the wall. But it ends, three minutes later, a bit after 6:00.

PROP PROBLEMS

Props can be both the *bête noire* of the filmmaker and a treasure trove for an alert flub-spotter. The term "props" (originally "properties") covers a wide range of items, from the physical things that an actor carries into a scene ("hand props," such as guns and knives) to bottles and glasses and the little gewgaws and tschatschkes ("set dressing") that add atmosphere and verisimilitude to the set.

Since most props aren't nailed down, there's always a chance that they can make an inadvertent move between one shot and another, causing a "jump" on the screen; they can be overlooked when the set is re-dressed from one scene to another, thus disappearing in the next shot; or something can happen from shot to shot that creates a noticeable change, such as the level of liquid in a bottle coming and going. They can even be the source of anachronisms, when the set decorator isn't watching his p's and q's.

Such was the case in *Mommie Dearest* (1981) when little Tina Crawford is at the bar, fixing a drink for one of her "uncles." On a counter can be seen a bottle of "Fantastik" cleaner, a product that certainly wasn't around in the late forties, the era of that particular scene. Prop problem.

In the controversial *Basic Instinct* (1992), as Michael Douglas and George Dzundza talk in a diner, the cap from a ketchup bottle is dropped and rattles onto the table. Next shot, it's back on the bottle again, even though neither of the two retrieved it. But someone on the prop crew must have fixed it between the two shots. Prop problem.

Dogging Tea and Sympathy

A pair of china dogs are back to back in a master shot (overall wide view) of a scene in Vincente Minnelli's *Tea and Sympathy* (1956). But when the camera moves in for close-ups, the dogs are face to face.

O.K. You Count It!

In *The Thomas Crown Affair* (1968), the haul from the first bank robbery totals $2,660,527.62, as explained by the police. It is broken down into 16,240 $20 bills, 19,871 $10 bills, 34,645 $5 bills, and 129,000 $1 bills, adding up to only $825,735, as later detailed by a secretary. That, of course, makes the whole greater than the sum of its parts.

The Fifth Wheel (and the Sixth)

It's one of filmdom's most memorable chase scenes—Steve McQueen's race up and down the hills of San Francisco in *Bullitt* (1968). Notice that during the course of the chase, the Dodge Charger which McQueen pursues loses three hubcaps. but when it crashes into a wall at the chase's end, three (more) hubcaps fly through the air.

Of course, such chases have to be carefully choreographed in order to look realistic. Even though they're usually shot on empty streets very early in the morning, extras drive other cars through the scenes to add verisimilitude. But notice how the same little Volkswagen bug keeps coming into the *Bullitt* chase scene time after time. Speedy little dude, isn't it?

Bouncing Boulders

If you've ever been on a movie studio tour, you've seen the foam-rubber boulders that are often used to prevent damage to actors in landslide scenes and the like. The fake boulders can look very real—unless they bounce. In *Raiders of the Lost Ark* (1981), watch as Harrison Ford shoves a boulder out of the escape hatchway. Then watch as the shadow of the boulder bounces.

...Wobbling Walls

And in a similar vein, in *The Jewel of the Nile* (1985), Michael Douglas does a Tarzan rope-swing into a rock wall, which "gives" as he hits it.

Trading Up

Patrick Swayze gives a paperback copy of Diana Vreeland's autobiography to a shop clerk when he and his fellow *To Wong Fu, Thanks for Everything, Julie Newmar* (1995) drag queens are stranded in a small town. Later, when the clerk reads the book, it has magically become a hard cover.

Thirty Days Hath...

A calendar on the wall in *Stars Fell On Henrietta* (1995) shows April with 31 days.

Just a Little (False) Note

Songbird Jeanette MacDonald pens a note in Victor Herbert's period musical *Naughty Marietta* (1935). But she writes it with a modern fountain pen.

Those Magnificent Yet-to-Be-Built Automobiles

The car that Steve Railsback drives in *The Stunt Man* (1980) is identified in dialogue as a Duesenberg, one of the most luxurious cars ever made. The car crashes through a bridge railing and into the river in a scene set in 1917. However, the first Duesenberg wasn't built until 1920.

Roses Are Red, Carnations Aren't

Business executive Katharine Hepburn leaves her high-rise office in the 1957 comedy *Desk Set*, carrying a bouquet of white carnations. Wonder what happened in the elevator on the way down? When she emerges into the building's lobby, the flowers have become pink.

So Maybe the Insurance Replaced It

Early in *Leaving Las Vegas* (1995) Nicholas Cage's character loses his wedding ring to a very talented hooker—but a few scenes later, he's wearing the ring again.

Aw, Stuff It

The makers of *Terror in the Jungle* (1968) used stuffed animals to simulate the real thing in several scenes—but weren't consistent. A stuffed lion in one scene becomes a stuffed tiger in another, and the stuffed tiger becomes a real tiger.

Medical Marvels

A doctor noticed that when an attorney holds up an X ray film during the Nazi trial in *The Man in the Glass Booth* (1975), it's supposed to show the defendant's shoulder. However, the X ray is of a woman's pelvis, with an intrauterine device (IUD) in place.

You've Seen One, You've Seen Them All

During the course of *Triple Cross* (1967), the luxury liner *Lusitania* is sunk. The ship pictured on the front of a newspaper reporting the event has two stacks. The *Lusitania* had four.

The Self-Setting Table

Denzel Washington places a couple of bowls on the edge of a table in *Philadelphia* (1993), then goes into the kitchen to talk to his wife. When he comes back into the dining room, the bowls have magically placed themselves atop plates.

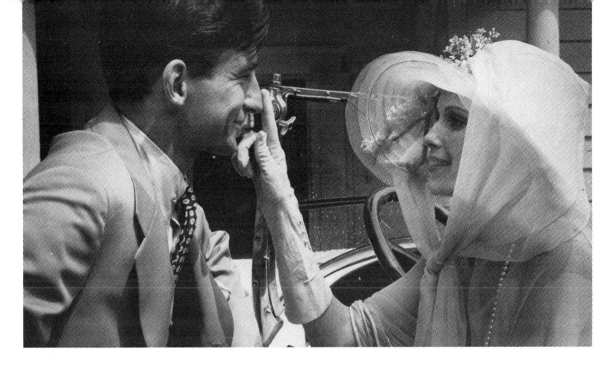

Of the Period...or Not?

The Great Gatsby (1974) is a lush period piece...and antique cars add much to the film's authenticity—except when a 1934 Packard cruises by in a scene set in 1925. Robert Young, Jr., spotted the error, and he should know. The Packard was his own car, a custom-crafted Super Eight Dual-Cowl Sports Sedan.

Another Glass of Milk, Please

When Dick Tracy and Tess Trueheart are in the diner with The Kid in *Dick Tracy* (1990), The Kid finishes a glass of milk, then runs for the door. Tracy puts him back in his seat, during which time the glass has magically refilled itself.

Maybe It Was Just a Very Wealthy Tribe

Near the end of *Outrageous Fortune* (1987), a handful of money is thrown from a cliff, to be gathered up by a tribe of Indians. But there are those who couldn't wait. If you look closely, before the dough is tossed, some of the Indians already have wads of the prop money stuffed in their pockets.

The Wreath That Wouldn't Go Away

One of Leonard Maltin's discoveries as revealed on "Entertainment Tonight" is Jimmy Stewart's problem with a wreath in *It's a Wonderful Life* (1946). He comes into the newspaper office carrying a wreath on his arm and tosses it casually aside, and picks up the phone. In the next shot, the wreath has popped back onto his arm.

Outreach and Touch Someone

We're not so sure that the prop makers and the set crew were communicating on *Scrooged* (1988). Karen Allen hands Bill Murray her business card, which reads "Operation Reachout." But when Murray calls on her at work, the sign on the building reads "Operation Outreach."

The Perils of Pearls

When going to visit Jessica Tandy at the nursing home for what turns out to be the last time in *Fried Green Tomatoes* (1991), Kathy Bates is wearing an off-white dress and a strand of pearls. In the next shot, the pearls are gone; they're back again when she arrives in the hospital room, then they vanish once more.

Make a Good Impression—And Save a Few Bucks

Michael Douglas does a nice sleight of hand in *Romancing the Stone* (1984) showing that his character is pretty cheap. He takes a very elaborate necklace out of his pocket and hands it to Kathleen Turner. But when she takes it, it's a simple charm on a chain.

Did Anyone Videotape It?

Demi Moore and Rob Lowe are making out in a jeep in *St. Elmo's Fire* (1985) when things get so hot that her long dangling earrings come and go several times.

Did Anyone Videotape It?: II

Andie McDowell wears a necklace when she's sitting in a chair and asking her husband if he's having an affair, in *sex, lies and videotape* (1989). Then she lays down in bed, still wearing the necklace. But moments later, it's gone.

Come Flub With Me

In the *Superman* parody which is part of *Hot Shots!* (1991)—itself a parody of *Top Gun*—watch as Charlie Sheen and Valeria Golino fly over the city. Her right earring, visible in the long shots, disappears in the close-ups. Since we're dealing with a parody within a parody from within the oh-so-warped mind of ZAZ's Jim Abrahams, is this a real flub or a parody of a flub—e.g., Yul Brynner's disappearing earring in *The King and I* (1956)? Your call.

So What Did She Use for Air?

In *Superman IV: The Quest for Peace* (1987), Nuclear Man (Mark Pillow) kidnaps Lacy Warfield (Mariel Hemingway) and takes her into outer space where she seems to have no trouble breathing—even without a space suit.

INSIDE JOKES

Ever since Alfred Hitchcock started the business of making cameo appearances in his own films—perhaps even before—directors, writers, and actors have loved to slip little "inside jokes" into their movies. More often than not, they're either subtle tributes or gentle digs at their friends in the business, references to their own earlier works, sight gags, or unbilled cameos of themselves and their buddies.

An inside joke can fit into the definition of a film flub—something that adds a quick dose of reality to the fantasy which is being played out on the screen—but unlike the accidents and oversights which make up most of the *FILM FLUBS* collections, inside jokes are intentional and deliberate.

Steven Spielberg and George Lucas love the in-joke so much that often they seem to trade little tributes to each other's work. Spielberg's *Indiana Jones and the Temple of Doom* (1984) opens with a sequence in Hong Kong's Club Obi-Wan. Think about it. In *Raiders of the Lost Ark* (1981) Indy is rescued by a seaplane bearing the license number OB-CPO, a nudge at the *Star Wars* characters. Also in *Raiders* there's an in-joke you'll have to look for in the movie houses, since it's too small to be seen on video. But when the Ark is moved, C3PO and R2D2 supposedly appear in the hieroglyphics on the Wall of Souls.

In *Close Encounters of the Third Kind* (1977) a minuscule R2D2 is built into the superstructure of the mothership. Spielberg is also fond of recalling his earlier works, as in *Gremlins* (1984). He executive-produced the film, and on a theater marquee could be seen the titles *A Boy's Life* and *Watch the Skies*—the working titles for *E. T. The Extra-Terrestrial* and *Close Encounters of the Third Kind*.

George Lucas isn't above the in-joke, too. The license plate number in *American Graffiti* (1973) is "THX-1138," the title of Lucas's first feature (and also the patronym of THX, his theatrical sound system). A cell block in *Star Wars* (1977) bears the same number. It's apparently meaningless. Lucas told an interviewer he just likes the sound of it.

There seems to be a bit of an in-joke in *Return of the Jedi* (1983). An alert viewer spotted a flying shoe in outer space. During a battle scene, Lando looks up from his controls and out of the Falcon's window a shoe moves from top left to bottom right. We've heard that there's a lot of garbage in outer space. Is Lucas confirming that for us?

"See You" in the Movies

Director John Landis likes to slip the phrase "See you next Wednesday" in his movies. It pops up in *Kentucky Fried Movie* (1977), *The Blues Brothers* (1980), *An American Werewolf in London* (1981), *Amazon Women on the Moon* (1987), and *Coming to America* (1988). The phrase is written in blood in the Landis-directed Michael Jackson video, *Thriller* (1984). Landis himself becomes the butt of a sick in-joke in *Wired* (1989). As the actor portraying the director walks across *The Blues Brothers* set, the sound of helicopters can be heard in the background. If you don't know what that's referring to, you don't know movies.

Targeting the Critics

On the set of *Willow* (1988), the two-headed monster was known as the "Ebersisk," a reference to Siskel and Ebert, even though the name didn't appear in the film. But critic Pauline Kael was speared in the same film by having the Evil General Kael bear her name.

The Road to the Circus

When Dorothy Lamour appears on-screen in *The Greatest Show on Earth* (1952), her "Road" buddies Bob Hope and Bing Crosby are sitting among the popcorn munching crowd on the circus bleachers.

Doing It Like a Rabbit

Some animation fans think that a quickie inside joke was drawn into *The Wabbit Who Came to Dinner*. In a scene where Bugs emerges from the shower and wraps a towel around himself (itself a bit of an oddity since he usually didn't wear clothes), there's a frame or two where an added bit of anatomy that you don't see in other "Bugs" cartoons seems to appear between his legs.

The Subliminal Dig

In John Carpenter's debut film, *Dark Star* (1974), for a brief moment on one of the computer screens appears the message, "Fuck You, Harris." Seems Carpenter didn't get along too well with the film's producer, Jack H. Harris.

Everybody Has to Start Somewhere

In *Bananas* (1971) look for an unknown player to practice his pugilistic skills by mugging Woody Allen on a New York subway. The same actor gets his just desserts in *Prisoner of Second Avenue* (1975), when, as an alleged pickpocket, he's mugged by Jack Lemmon. The neophyte bit player is Sylvester Stallone.

Paying Homage to the Family

Among the names which Dustin Hoffman memorizes and recites in *Rain Man* (1988) are Marsha and William Gottsegen—in real life, Hoffman's in-laws.

Paying Homage to One's Self

A radio station employee in Oliver Stone's *Talk Radio* (1988) reads a copy of *Playboy* which features an interview with...Oliver Stone.

Paying Homage to One's Work

Child actors sing the theme from Alan Parker's *Fame* (1980) and a poster featuring Parker's *Pink Floyd—The Wall* (1982) appears in Parker's *Shoot the Moon* (1982). Incidentally, *The Wall* wasn't released until five months after *Shoot the Moon*. But Parker isn't the only one. In *Lethal Weapon* (1987) Richard Donner advertises his upcoming movie with a theater marquee in the background which reads "*The Lost Boys*—This Year's Hit."

Paying Homage to the Progenitors

In *2010* (1984), the man feeding the pigeons on a park bench outside the White House is *2001/2010* writer Arthur C. Clarke. Clarke also appears on the cover of *Time* magazine as the President of the United States, alongside another familiar face as premier of the USSR—director Stanley Kubrick.

Kubrick himself pulls off an in-joke by displaying a copy of the *2001: A Space Odyssey* sound track in a record shop in *A Clockwork Orange* (1971).

While we're on the subject, did you know that the very date in *2001* that the computer HAL says that he became operational is itself a flub? Hal says that it was January 12, 1992—but in an interview published on that date, Clarke himself says that it was a flub.

He told the *Los Angeles Times* "...the strange thing is that in the book it's 1997—not 1992—and I have no idea when the change occurred, whether Stanley [Kubrick] changed it in the screenplay [coauthored by Clarke] or the actor flubbed his line."

Welcome, Mr. Clarke, to our Blue-Ribbon Flub Spotter Panel.

Homage to One's Own Work: The Sequel

When the camera tracks down a New York street in *Ghostbusters II* (1989), notice the theater marquee advertising *Cannibal Girls* starring director Ivan Reitman's buddies Eugene Levy and Andrea Martin. The advertised movie was a 1973 Canadian cheapie, an early effort of Reitman, Levy, and Martin.